Olivia

COMPLETE
EnglishSmart ®

GRADE **4**

Olivia

Section 1	Listening Comprehension	

Unit 1 6 – 9
The Human Heart

Unit 2 10 – 13
Education in the Renaissance

Unit 3 14 – 17
J. K. Rowling – Her Story

Unit 4 18 – 21
The Atlas

Unit 5 22 – 25
Medieval Castles

Review 1 26 – 31

Section 2	Grammar

Unit 1 34 – 37
Common and Proper Nouns

Unit 2 38 – 41
Subjects and Objects

Unit 3 42 – 45
Pronouns

Unit 4 46 – 49
Verb Tenses

Unit 5 50 – 53
Adjectives

Unit 6 54 – 57
Adverbs

Unit 7 58 – 61
Prepositions

Unit 8 62 – 65
Conjunctions

Unit 9 66 – 69
The Sentence: Subject and Predicate

Unit 10 70 – 73
Subject-verb Agreement

Unit 11 74 – 77
Simple, Compound, and Complex Sentences

Unit 12 78 – 81
Phrases and Clauses

Unit 13 82 – 85
More on Phrases

Unit 14 86 – 89
Punctuation

Review 2 90 – 95

Section 3	Vocabulary

Unit 1 98 – 101
Adaptation Words

Unit 2 102 – 105
Medical Words

Unit 3 106 – 109
Herbal Medicine Words

Unit 4 110 – 113
Brain Words

Contents

Grade 4

Unit 5   114 – 117
Canadian Words

Unit 6   118 – 121
Toy and Game Words

Unit 7   122 – 125
Ancient Civilization Words

Unit 8   126 – 129
Money Words

Unit 9   130 – 133
Knight Words

Unit 10   134 – 137
Weather Words

Unit 11   138 – 141
Sport Words

Unit 12   142 – 145
Gardening Words

Unit 13   146 – 149
Musical Instrument Words

Unit 14   150 – 153
Technology Words

Review 3   154 – 159

Section 4   Reading and Writing

Unit 1   162 – 165
Not a Typical Grandma

Unit 2   166 – 169
Camp Wannastay

Unit 3   170 – 173
The Father, the Son, and the Donkey

Unit 4   174 – 177
A Pet's Tale

Unit 5   178 – 181
A Rebus Invitation

Unit 6   182 – 185
New France – the Beginning of Canada

Unit 7   186 – 189
Seal Island

Unit 8   190 – 193
The Production of Milk

Unit 9   194 – 197
Salamanders

Unit 10   198 – 201
Disasters at Sea

Unit 11   202 – 205
The Case of the Disappearing Fish

Unit 12   206 – 209
Being the Eldest

Unit 13   210 – 213
Nature's Fireworks

Unit 14   214 – 217
Stonehenge

Review 4   218 – 223

Listening Scripts   225 – 230

Answers   231 – 256

Language Games   257 – 272

Dear Parent,

Thank you for choosing our *Complete EnglishSmart* as your child's learning companion.

We are confident that *Complete EnglishSmart* is the ultimate supplementary workbook your child needs to build his or her English language skills.

Complete EnglishSmart explores the fundamental aspects of language development – listening comprehension, grammar, vocabulary, reading, and writing – by introducing each concept with an easy-to-understand definition and clear examples. This is followed by a variety of interesting activities to provide plenty of practice for your child. There is also a note box at the end of each unit for your child to note down what he or she has learned.

To further ensure that your child retains the language concepts and enjoys the material, there is a review at the end of each section and a Language Games section at the end of the book to help your child consolidate the language concepts in a fun and meaningful way. The accompanying online audio clips let your child practise and develop his or her listening skills.

If your child would like to show his or her understanding of the language concepts in a creative way, we are happy to invite your child on a bonus Language Game Design Challenge. Please find the detailed information on page 271 of this book.

We hope that your child will have fun learning and developing his or her English language skills with our *Complete EnglishSmart*.

Your Partner in Education,
Popular Book Company (Canada) Limited

Don't forget to participate in our
Language Game Design Challenge *on
p. 271 for your chance to win a prize!*

Section 1

Listening Comprehension

UNIT 1

The Human Heart

 This passage explains general facts about the powerful human heart. You will learn what the heart does, what makes up the heart, how the heart works, and what happens to your heart when you perform physical action. You will learn how incredible the human heart is.

my heart

1.1 Read the questions in this unit before listening. Take notes as you listen. You may read the listening script on page 225 if needed.

Keywords	Notes
involuntary	
blood vessel	
incredible	
muscle	
chamber	
atrium	
ventricle	
heartbeat	
consistently	
valve	
exhausted	
oxygen reserve	
resume	
heart rate	

A. Read the questions. Then check the correct answers.

1. How big is the human heart?

   (A) the same size as our head
   (B) about the size of a fist
   (C) the size of a watermelon
   (D) as big as a ping pong ball

2. What are the chambers of the heart called?

   (A) valves
   (B) atriums and ventricles
   (C) lungs
   (D) vessels

3. What is the typical heart rate of a child?

   (A) 50 – 60 beats per minute
   (B) 60 – 80 beats per minute
   (C) 80 – 100 beats per minute
   (D) 100 – 110 beats per minute

4. After exercising, why do you feel exhausted?

   (A) Your blood stops circulating.
   (B) Your lungs stop working.
   (C) Your oxygen reserve is used up.
   (D) The valves in your heart stop working.

B. Listen to the questions and answer options. Then write the correct letters in the boxes.

1.2

1

2

3

4

C.   Fill in the blanks with the correct words to complete the sentences.

> valves   oxygen   muscle   chambers   vessels

1.   The heart is an involuntary _____ .

2.   The heart sends blood through blood _____ to all parts of your body.

3.   There are four _____ in the human heart.

4.   Blood goes from the heart to the lungs to load up on _____ .

5.   The heart has _____ that open and shut with the flow of blood.

D.   Answer the questions.

1.   What are the different parts of the heart? What do they do?

_____

_____

_____

2.   Explain what a single heartbeat does to your body.

_____

_____

_____

3.   What happens to your heart when you run?

_____

_____

_____

E. **Listen to the passage "The Human Heart" again. Then write a summary in no more than 80 words.**

1.1

Include only the main points in the summary. Use your own words.

Summary

_____

_____

_____

_____

_____

_____

_____

_____

Words **that I Have Learned**

_____

_____

_____

_____

UNIT

2 Education in the Renaissance

 This passage explains general facts about education in the Renaissance Period (1500 – 1650). You will learn how people studied, what they studied, who could go to university, and the different types of education. You will learn how the Renaissance Period was an exciting time for scholars.

 2.1 Read the questions in this unit before listening. Take notes as you listen. You may read the listening script on page 226 if needed.

Keywords	Notes
ancient	
philosophy	
century	
privilege	
handwritten	
establish	
scholar	
conduct	
experiment	
mystery	
universe	
publish	
theory	
invention	

A. **Read the questions. Then check the correct answers.**

1. Who could attend university?

   Ⓐ girls   Ⓑ the poor

   Ⓒ anyone   Ⓓ the rich

2. How were books made in the Renaissance Period?

   Ⓐ They were printed.

   Ⓑ They were handwritten.

   Ⓒ They were etched.

   Ⓓ Books did not exist then.

3. Who supported Copernicus's discovery about the Earth and the sun?

   Ⓐ the Greek   Ⓑ the Church

   Ⓒ Galileo   Ⓓ all scholars

4. What was an invention from the Renaissance Period?

   Ⓐ the telescope

   Ⓑ the computer

   Ⓒ the telephone

   Ⓓ the train

B. **Listen to the questions and answer options. Then write the correct letters in the boxes.**

2.2

①

②

③

④

C.   Write "T" for the true statements and "F" for the false ones.

1.   Many universities were founded during the Renaissance Period.   _____

2.   One had to speak French to go to university in France.   _____

3.   During the Renaissance Period, university tests were written.   _____

4.   In school, only teachers had books.   _____

5.   Poor children could study the Bible in grammar schools.   _____

6.   The submarine was a Renaissance invention.   _____

D.   Answer the questions.

1.   Why were so many universities founded during the Renaissance Period?

    _____

    _____

    _____

2.   What were some of the inventions from the Renaissance Period?

    _____

    _____

3.   Why was Copernicus afraid to publish his works on his discovery?

    _____

    _____

    _____

E. Listen to the passage "Education in the Renaissance" again. Then write a summary in no more than 80 words.

2.1

Include only the main points in the summary. Use your own words.

Summary

_____

_____

_____

_____

_____

_____

_____

_____

_____

Words that I Have Learned

_____

_____

_____

_____

UNIT

3

J. K. Rowling – Her Story

This passage tells the story of how J. K. Rowling became the successful author of the Harry Potter novels. You will learn what her life was like before writing the Harry Potter series, why she became a writer, and how she created the bestselling novel series.

3.1

Read the questions in this unit before listening. Take notes as you listen. You may read the listening script on page 227 if needed.

Keywords	Notes
success	
fantasy	
series	
phenomenon	
fame	
social assistance	
novel	
literature	
occupation	
character	
source	
author	
credit	

A. Read the questions. Then check the correct answers.

1. How many copies of the Harry Potter books have been sold worldwide?

(A) hundreds
(B) thousands
(C) tens of thousands
(D) millions

2. Where did J. K. Rowling write her first Harry Potter book?

(A) in a public library
(B) in a nearby park
(C) in her apartment
(D) in a local café

3. The first Harry Potter book is titled *Harry Potter and* _____ .

(A) *the Prisoner of Azkaban*
(B) *the Goblet of Fire*
(C) *the Sorcerer's Stone*
(D) *the Chamber of Secrets*

4. Where do the odd names in the Harry Potter books come from?

(A) suggestions from readers
(B) a variety of sources
(C) people J. K. Rowling knows
(D) They are all made up.

B. Listen to the questions and answer options. Then write the correct letters in the boxes.

3.2

1

2

3

4

C.   Match the two parts and write the letters on the lines.

A J. K. Rowling's life
B a modern-day phenomenon
C because of Harry Potter
D since she was a child
E when she was six

1.   The success of the Harry Potter books is _____ .

2.   J. K. Rowling wrote her first story _____ .

3.   J. K. Rowling loved English literature _____ .

4.   The stories of Harry Potter are not based on _____ .

5.   Children are more interested in reading _____ .

D.   Answer the questions.

1.   Why did J. K. Rowling want to become a writer?

_____

_____

2.   How did J. K. Rowling come up with the characters in the Harry Potter stories?

_____

_____

3.   Why do you think J. K. Rowling has been credited with increasing children's interest in reading worldwide?

_____

_____

E. **Listen to the passage "J. K. Rowling – Her Story" again. Then write a summary in no more than 80 words.**

3.1

Include only the main points in the summary. Use your own words.

Summary

_____

_____

_____

_____

_____

_____

_____

_____

Words that I Have Learned

_____

_____

_____

_____

UNIT 4

The Atlas

 This passage explains general facts about atlases. You will learn what an atlas is, what is on an atlas, and how it helps us. You will learn why the atlas is important for us.

4.1 **Read the questions in this unit before listening. Take notes as you listen. You may read the listening script on page 228 if needed.**

Keywords	Notes
scale model	
land mass	
continent	
ocean	
imaginary	
globe	
equator	
Greenwich	
prime meridian	
latitude	
parallel	
longitude	
meridian	
degree	

A. Read the questions. Then check the correct answers.

1. What is a continent?

   Ⓐ a large land mass   Ⓑ a globe

   Ⓒ a large body of water   Ⓓ an imaginary circle

2. What is the imaginary line that circles the globe halfway between the North Pole and the South Pole called?

   Ⓐ the equator

   Ⓑ the prime meridian

   Ⓒ Greenwich

   Ⓓ the degree

3. How many minutes are there in a degree?

   Ⓐ 44   Ⓑ 60

   Ⓒ 90   Ⓓ 180

4. Lines of longitude are imaginary lines that run _____ .

   Ⓐ east-west

   Ⓑ north-south

   Ⓒ between the two poles

   Ⓓ parallel to the equator

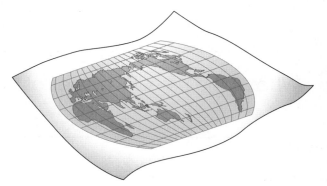

B. Listen to the questions and answer options. Then write the correct letters in the boxes.

 4.2

 **1**

 **2**

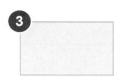 **3**

 **4**

C.   List the seven continents and five oceans.

Seven Continents
_____
_____
_____
_____
_____

Five Oceans
_____
_____
_____
_____
_____

D.   Answer the questions.

1.   What is the prime meridian?

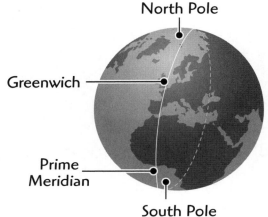

North Pole

Greenwich

Prime
Meridian

South Pole

_____

_____

_____

2.   What is the use of the lines of latitude and the lines of longitude?

_____

_____

_____

3.   What are parallels? Why are they called parallels?

_____

_____

_____

E. **Listen to the passage "The Atlas" again. Then write a summary in no more than 80 words.**

4.1

> Include only the main points in the summary. Use your own words.

Summary

_____

_____

_____

_____

_____

_____

_____

_____

Words that I Have Learned

_____

_____

_____

_____

UNIT 5 Medieval Castles

This passage explains general facts about castles in medieval times. You will learn why castles were built, what was inside castles, and what castles were like then and now. You will learn how things have changed since medieval times.

5.1 Read the questions in this unit before listening. Take notes as you listen. You may read the listening script on page 229 if needed.

Keywords	Notes
lord	
inhabitant	
apartment	
furnish	
protection	
lease	
defend	
invader	
maintain	
noble	
expense	
employ	
battle	
convert	

A. Read the questions. Then check the correct answers.

1. Who occupied castles?

    Ⓐ villagers   Ⓑ lords and ladies

    Ⓒ farmers   Ⓓ guests

2. Castles had many _____ .

    Ⓐ bedrooms   Ⓑ schools

    Ⓒ libraries   Ⓓ chapels

3. A noble in medieval times would have an income of about
    _____ .

    Ⓐ £1000   Ⓑ £2500

    Ⓒ £10 000   Ⓓ £1 000 000

4. How much might an ordinary working person in medieval
    times earn?

    Ⓐ a dollar a day

    Ⓑ a dollar a week

    Ⓒ a dollar a month

    Ⓓ a dollar a year

**B. Listen to the questions and answer options. Then write the correct letters in
the boxes.**

5.2

 ❶

 ❷

 ❸

 ❹

C.   Fill in the blanks with the correct words to complete the sentences.

1.   The main purpose of a castle was _____ .

2.   Bedrooms in castles had huge _____ beds and thick curtains to prevent _____ .

3.   In castles, the main heat source came from _____ .

4.   Farmers who leased land from a lord paid him _____ with farm _____ .

5.   In the late 1500s, castles were no longer needed because _____ became large-scale events.

D.   Answer the questions.

1.   Describe the inside of a medieval castle.

   _____

   _____

   _____

2.   Why were villages established near a castle?

   _____

   _____

3.   Why were castles expensive to run?

   _____

   _____

E. Listen to the passage "Medieval Castles" again. Then write a summary in no more than 80 words.

5.1

> Include only the main points in the summary. Use your own words.

Summary

_____

_____

_____

_____

_____

_____

_____

_____

_____

Words that I Have Learned

_____

_____

_____

_____

The Incredible Butterfly

This passage explains the characteristics of butterflies. You will learn about their appearance, what they eat, how they eat, how they ward off their predators, and how they turn from an egg to a caterpillar to a butterfly. You will learn about their life cycle and where these beautiful creatures can be found.

R1.1   **Read the questions in this review before listening. Take notes as you listen. You may read the listening script on page 230 if needed.**

Notes

A. Circle the answers.

1. How do butterflies camouflage themselves?

   They hide.

   They use their colours.

   They fly away.

2. What does a proboscis look like?

   a long mouth

   a long nose

   a long tongue

3. What is the purpose of the proboscis?

   to make mating calls

   to shoot poison at predators

   to suck up nectar

4. Which butterfly is this?

   the Painted Lady

   the Magnificent Owl

   the Monarch

5. In the pupa stage, the caterpillar changes into a/an _____ .

   egg

   chrysalis

   butterfly

6. How many weeks does it take for the egg to hatch?

   two weeks

   three weeks

   four weeks

7. Where are most butterflies found?

   in tropical climates

   in Australia

   in Antarctica

8. Which is the most widely distributed butterfly?

   the Painted Lady

   the Painted Owl

   the Magnificent Owl

B.   Listen to the questions and answer options. Then write the correct letters in the boxes.

R1.2

1 ⬜   **2** ⬜   **3** ⬜   **4** ⬜

C.   Label the diagram to show the order of the life cycle of a butterfly.

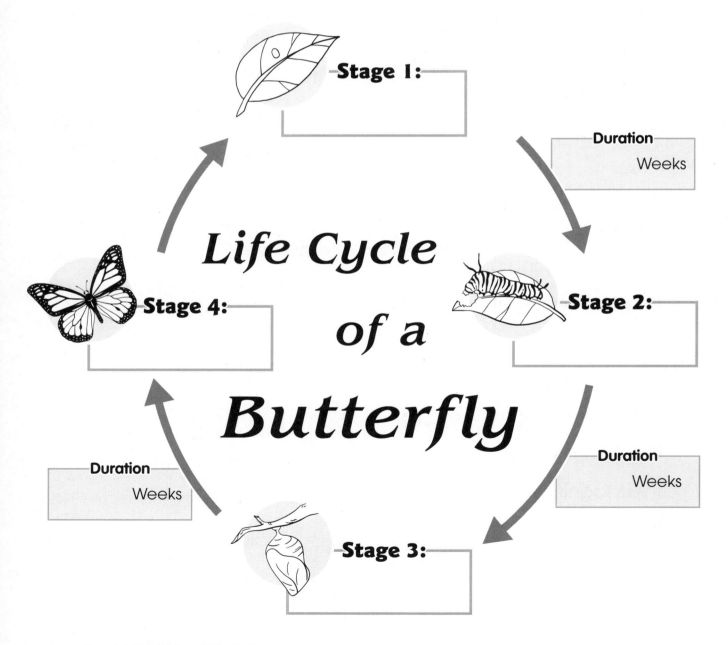

Stage 1:

Duration
Weeks

Stage 2:

Duration
Weeks

Stage 3:

Stage 4:

Duration
Weeks

Life Cycle of a Butterfly

D. **Rewrite the sentences as they are in the passage "The Incredible Butterfly".**

1. They are able to blend with three branches or flowers they feed.

    _____

2. Butterflies are important to nurture because they pollute plants when they feed.

    _____

    _____

3. The pupa stage is where the carpenter challenges into a butterfly.

    _____

    _____

E. **Match the descriptions with the correct pictures. Write the letters in the circles.**

A. the Painted Lady

B. an artist painting butterflies

C. the Magnificent Owl

D. a butterfly using its proboscis

E. a butterfly using its colour to camouflage

F. a butterfly using its colour to warn predators

F.   Fill in the blanks with the correct words to complete the sentences.

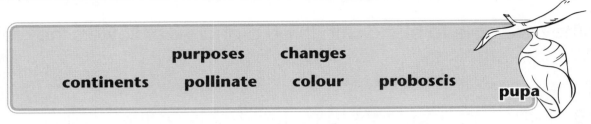

purposes   changes

continents   pollinate   colour   proboscis

pupa

1.   While admired by artists, the colours of butterflies serve other

_____ .

2.   The Painted Lady can be found on all _____ except
Australia and Antarctica.

3.   Butterflies _____ plants when they feed.

4.   Butterflies go through many _____ in both body form and

_____ .

5.   The _____ is a long mouthpart that butterflies use to dip
into flowers and suck up nectar.

6.   _____ is another word for chrysalis.

G.   Colour the continents where the Painted Lady can be found.

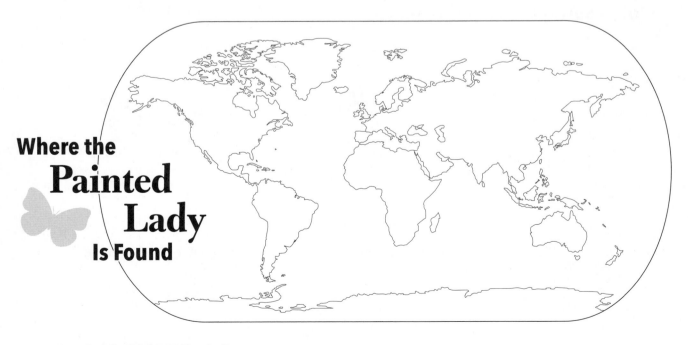

Where the
Painted
Lady
Is Found

H. Answer the questions.

1. How do butterflies use their colours to protect themselves against predators?

_____

_____

_____

2. Describe the life cycle of the butterfly.

_____

_____

_____

R1.1

I. Listen to the passage "The Incredible Butterfly" again. Then write a summary in no more than 80 words.

Listen carefully to make sure you catch all the important points of the passage to include in your summary. Use your own words.

_____

_____

_____

_____

_____

_____

_____

_____

Complete EnglishSmart (Grade 4)

Section 2

Grammar

UNIT

1

Common and Proper Nouns

A **common noun** names a general person, place, thing, or animal.

A **proper noun** names a specific person, place, thing, or animal. All proper nouns begin with a capital letter.

Examples

		Common Noun	Proper Noun
👶	person	doctor	Dr. Bryans
🏠	place	city	Toronto
✂️	thing	computer	Mac Book
🐰	animal	dog	Poodle

A.   Read each sentence. Circle the proper noun for the underlined common noun.

1. Marie Antoinette was the last <u>queen</u> of France.

2. Amy lives in a <u>neighbourhood</u> called Rosedale.

3. My parents bought me a <u>dog</u>. It is a Shih Tzu.

4. We will have dinner with Aunt Nellie at Taste Magic, the new <u>restaurant</u> in the nearby plaza.

5. The largest <u>continent</u> in the world is Asia.

6. Stonehenge is a ring of giant standing <u>stones</u> in England.

7. Our family <u>doctor</u>, Dr. Spinelli, is great!

8. The Golden Gate Bridge is a very famous <u>bridge</u>.

9. The Yangtze is a <u>river</u> that drains into the East China Sea.

10. Brianna is my favourite <u>character</u> in this story.

Many **proper nouns** are long. They are often titles and names, like book or movie titles and names of sports teams.

 The Wizard of Oz

 The Toronto Blue Jays

B. **Fill in the blanks with the correct proper nouns.**

> **The Lion King**   **Toronto Maple Leafs**
>
> **Empire State Building**   **Art Gallery of Ontario**
>
> **Great Pyramid of Giza**   **The Chronicles of Narnia**
>
> **Where the Wild Things Are**

1. The _____ in New York City is 102 stories tall.

2. The _____ is a beautiful building in Toronto.

3. _____ is an interesting children's picture book.

4. My dad bought us tickets to see my favourite team, the _____ .

5. _____ is a book series written by C. S. Lewis.

6. _____ is a famous animated film.

7. The _____ is among the Seven Wonders of the World.

Section 2

Grammar

Examples

A common noun can be countable or uncountable.

Countable nouns are things that we can count using numbers. They have plural forms (usually formed by adding "s" or "es").

Uncountable nouns are things that we cannot count using numbers. They do not have plural forms.

Common Nouns

countable
book
book**s**

uncountable
snow

C. **Put each noun in the correct category. Then give one more example for each category.**

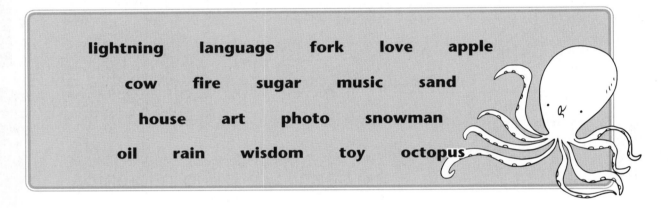

lightning   language   fork   love   apple

cow   fire   sugar   music   sand

house   art   photo   snowman

oil   rain   wisdom   toy   octopus

Countable Noun	**Uncountable Noun**
My example: _____	My example: _____

D. **Circle the correct nouns.**

> *Decide whether the nouns are countable or uncountable.*

1. Sara ate two pieces of **pie / pies** for lunch.

2. The students learned a lot of new **information / informations** in class.

3. Tim listens to **music / musics** as he does his homework.

4. Lester used more than a thousand **block / blocks** to build that tower!

5. Jane and Rebecca bought **popcorn / popcorns** before the movie.

6. The three siblings take turns to do the **dish / dishes** after dinner.

7. Remember to add no more than one teaspoon of **salt /salts** in the soup.

8. My sister likes using traditional handmade bar **soap / soaps** .

9. You can find lots of **seashell / seashells** on the beach.

Words that I Have Learned

Common Noun _____

Proper Noun _____

Countable Noun _____

Uncountable Noun _____

UNIT

2

Subjects and Objects

The **subject** of a verb is the person or thing that performs the action. It can be a noun or a pronoun.

The subject can also be the person or thing that is being described.

Examples

• <u>Ken</u> is reading the travel guide.
  └── subject doing the action

• <u>It</u> is very cute.
  └── subject being described

A. Circle the subject in each sentence.

1. Hannah loves dancing to the music.

2. The cat is chasing some squirrels in the garden.

3. Joey eats sandwiches for lunch almost every day.

4. We are going to the water park this coming Saturday.

5. Recycling is important for the environment.

6. The team's goal is to win the football game on Friday.

7. They are coming to my birthday party.

8. Kyle paid for the movie tickets last night.

9. My favourite teacher always tells us interesting stories.

10. The hockey players passed the puck around the rink.

The **object** of a verb is the person or thing that receives the action of the verb. It can be a noun or a pronoun.

Examples

- Mom bought <u>a ring</u> yesterday.
  ↑ noun

- The old lady asked <u>me</u> for help.
  ↑ pronoun

B.   Fill in the blanks with the correct objects.

1. Brandon plays the _____ in
    the school band.
    trumpet/phone

2. We watched the _____ at night.
    sun/stars

3. When you are in a car, you should always wear your
    _____ .
    cap/seat belt

4. Jaclyn loves eating _____ in the summer.
    ice cream/cups

5. I like _____ very much, especially science fiction.
    sports/books

6. The teacher can help _____ with the math
    questions.
    we/us

7. Lilah asked _____ for more dessert.
    they/her

8. The parents watched their _____ play soccer.
    children/students

9. Luke walked the _____ after school.
    dog/car

10. He likes to eat _____ with fries.
    burgers/milk

A **direct object** is the noun or pronoun that receives the action of the verb. Some sentences do not have objects.

Examples

- I wash <u>the dishes</u>.
  ↑
  └— direct object

- The baby cried. ← no object

C. Fill in the blanks with the correct direct objects. Then write two more sentences with direct objects to end the paragraph. Circle the direct objects.

| the room | herbs | them | gardening |
| the plants | many plants | some flowers |

My sister likes 1._____ . She

has grown 2._____ in the

backyard. They include fruit trees, flowers, and 3._____ .

She waters 4._____ every day. Her flowers are in different

colours: red, pink, white, and yellow. Sometimes, in the morning,

she cuts 5._____ and places 6._____ in the dining

room. They make 7._____ look beautiful. They smell sweet

too. _____

_____

_____

_____

| | Example |

An **indirect object** is the noun or pronoun to whom or to what the verb is directed.

Fred is building <u>Bobby</u> <u>a house</u>.

indirect object ⟶   direct object

D. **Write "D" if the underlined words are direct objects and "I" if they are indirect objects.**

1. Please lend <u>me</u> (   ) the book.

2. He gave Johnny <u>tickets</u> (   ) to the game.

3. Can you give him <u>a call</u> (   ) tomorrow?

4. The doctor gave <u>the patient</u> (   ) a prescription.

5. She told me <u>the truth</u> (   ).

6. The audience gave <u>the performer</u> (   ) a round of applause.

7. The nurse handed the dentist <u>the tool</u> (   ).

8. I gave <u>my friend</u> (   ) a gift.

Thank you!

Words that I Have Learned

_____

_____

_____

UNIT

3 Pronouns

A **pronoun** replaces a noun. It must agree in gender (male or female) and number (singular or plural) with the noun it replaces. It can be a subject or an object in a sentence.

Subject Pronoun

| I | you | we | they | he | she | it |

Object Pronoun

| me | you | us | them | him | her | it |

Examples

Mr. and Mrs. Green bought a yacht. <u>They</u> named <u>it</u> "Ruby".

replaces "Mr. and Mrs. Green"

refers to the "yacht"

Ruby

A. Fill in the blanks with the correct pronouns.

Bonnie and Jennifer are in my class. 1._____ are my best friends. 2._____ like skipping very much and I enjoy playing with 3._____ . Bonnie is the best player. 4._____ always wins. I can never beat 5._____ .

My younger brother and I love Halloween. Every year, Mom makes Halloween costumes for 6._____ . This year, she made a hat and a cloak for 7._____ . 8._____ will dress like a witch and take a broom with me. 9._____ made a tiger costume for my brother. 10._____ really suits 11._____ well because he always acts like a tiger. 12._____ will go around in our neighbourhood to get candies.

A **possessive pronoun** shows ownership or relationship. It is not followed by a noun.

Possessive Pronoun

mine	yours	ours
theirs	his	hers

Example

I've cleaned my room. Have you cleaned <u>yours</u>?

↑ possessive pronoun; referring to "your room"

Note that there is no need to put "room" after "yours".

B. Fill in the blanks with the correct possessive pronouns.

1. John, is this backpack _____ ?

2. Do you need a pencil? You can borrow _____ .

3. If we work as a team, the victory will be _____ !

4. I finished my homework. Did Ray and Liz finish _____ ?

C. Rewrite the sentences using possessive pronouns for the underlined words.

1. This is <u>my</u> cheese. This cheese is _____ .

2. This is <u>Jerry's</u> present. _____

3. These are <u>your</u> cards. _____

4. This is <u>my parents'</u> bed. _____

5. That is <u>Mary's</u> lunch box. _____

6. These are <u>my</u> photo albums. _____

7. This is <u>Pansy's and my</u> secret. _____

An **interrogative pronoun** asks a question. "Who", "what", "which", "whose", and "whom" are interrogative pronouns.

Examples

- <u>What</u> did you have for dinner?
- <u>Whose</u> are these? Are they Ivan's?

D. Circle the correct interrogative pronouns.

1. **Which / Whose** should I pick? They all look yummy.

2. To **whom / what** did you talk?

3. **Which / What** is wrong with your car?

4. **Whom / Whose** is this? Is it yours?

5. **What / Which** do you like, the cake or the pie?

6. **Which / Who** wants to come with me?

E. Underline the interrogative pronoun in each sentence. Check the circle if it is correct. If not, write the correct interrogative pronoun above it.

1. Which won the gold medal in the long jump?   ◯

2. Who has he done to make you angry?   ◯

3. With which would you like to dance?   ◯

4. I found this key. Whose is it?   ◯

5. Which is heavier, a bike or a car?   ◯

6. What brought this birthday cake?   ◯

F. Fill in the blanks with the correct interrogative pronouns.

1. _____ put my boot here?

2. _____ did he find in the box?

3. _____ took this scary picture?

4. _____ are these? Mine are over there.

5. _____ should I pick, the blue card or the red card?

6. _____ will you take to the concert?

7. _____ is the highest score? Is it Sarah's?

8. There are so many choices here. _____ have you chosen?

G. Write questions using the following interrogative pronouns.

1. Who _____

2. What _____

3. Which _____

4. Whose _____

5. Whom _____

Words that I Have Learned

Subject Pronoun _____

Object Pronoun _____

Possessive Pronoun _____

Interrogative Pronoun _____

UNIT
4 Verb Tenses

Verbs can be in different tenses. The **simple present tense** talks about facts, present actions, and habitual actions. Most present tense verbs for third person singular subjects are formed by adding "s" or "es" to the base form.

Example

Eric <u>rides</u> a bike to school.

A.   Fill in the blanks with the correct simple present tense verbs.

My mom 1._____ going out for dinner. She 2._____
likes/liked says/sayes

it 3._____ her a break from cooking. On Fridays, Dad
givs/gives

4._____ her to her favourite restaurant. Mom 5._____
takes/taks <div>trys/tries</div>

something new each week but Dad 6._____ pasta every time.
orders/orderes

Dad 7._____ eating there, too. He 8._____ the only
liks/likes <div>saies/says</div>

part he 9._____ 10._____ when it 11._____ time to
hats/hates <div>be/is</div> <div>is/are</div>

pay! When they 12._____ , a
goes/go

neighbour 13._____ my sister
watches/watchs

and me. We 14._____ games
play/plays

and 15._____ pizza.
eat/ate

The **simple past tense** talks about past actions. Most past tense verbs are formed by adding "d" or "ed" to the base form. Some past tense verbs have irregular endings.

Examples

help + ed

• We <u>helped</u> mom do the housework this morning.

• I <u>caught</u> a fish yesterday.

irregular ending

B. **Underline the verbs in the sentences. Then check if the verbs are in the simple past tense. If not, write the verbs in the simple past tense on the lines.**

Simple Past Tense

1. She speaks too loudly in the library. ◯ _____

2. The kettle whistled when the hot water boiled. ◯ _____

3. Jon writes me a short story. ◯ _____

4. It takes us three hours to get to the cottage. ◯ _____

5. Raindrops fell on my head as I walked home. ◯ _____

C. **Fill in the blanks with the simple past tense of the given verbs.**

Yesterday, Kara 1._____ (play) with Michelle during recess. They 2._____ (decide) to play catch. Joshua 3._____ (notice) them and 4._____ (ask) if he could join them. Joshua 5._____ (say) he 6._____ (use) to play catch a lot when he 7._____ (live) in Hawaii. The three friends 8._____ (keep) playing until the school bell 9._____ (ring).

The **simple future tense** talks about future actions. The verb is formed by adding "will" before the base form.

Jane <u>will sing</u> a song.

D. **Fill in the blanks with the correct verbs in the simple future tense.**

help

make

be

bring

come

1. Dad _____ home a treat for us.

2. Aunt Trudy _____ a pot of tea.

3. I _____ home in an hour.

4. The zoo _____ a lot of fun!

5. Annie _____ me with my homework.

E. **Rewrite the sentences by changing the underlined verbs to the simple future tense.**

1. I <u>see</u> many clowns at the circus.

   _____

   _____

2. The soccer game <u>is</u> exciting.

   _____

3. Lindsay <u>bakes</u> an apple pie tomorrow.

   _____

4. The Wilson family <u>goes</u> to Italy next week.

   _____

F. **Underline the verb in each sentence. Then write the verb in the correct tense above it.**

1. Gary returns the books to the library last Friday.

2. Maria goes to the musical with her friends tomorrow night.

3. Mom grew a lot of flowers every summer.

4. Don will not finish his homework in time for class yesterday.

5. Father's Day fell on the third Sunday of June.

6. We watch the sun set yesterday.

7. I show you the way afterwards.

8. The hurricane brings a lot of rain last week.

9. Was this watermelon sweet?

Words that I Have Learned

_____

_____

_____

UNIT

5 Adjectives

A **comparative adjective** compares two nouns. For an adjective with one syllable, the comparative form is formed by adding "er". For an adjective with two or more syllables, add "more" before the original adjective. Some adjectives have irregular comparative forms.

Examples

- The roses are <u>taller</u> than the tulips but the tulips are <u>more beautiful</u>.

- The weather today is <u>better</u> than yesterday's.

A. Circle the correct comparative form for each adjective.

1. comfortable   **comfortabler / more comfortable**

2. difficult   **difficulter / more difficult**

3. bad   **badder / worse**

4. easy   **easier / more easy**

5. bright   **brighter / more bright**

B. Check if the adjectives are in the comparative form. If not, write the correct comparative adjectives on the lines.

1. Walking uphill is tiring than going downhill. ⃝ _____

2. Sandra is more capable than Peggy. ⃝ _____

3. I am strong than you. ⃝ _____

4. Danielle is slimmer than her sister. ⃝ _____

5. This book is interesting than that book. ⃝ _____

A **superlative adjective** compares three or more nouns. For adjectives with one syllable, the superlative form is formed by adding "est". For adjectives with two or more syllables, add "most" before the original adjective. Some adjectives have irregular superlative forms.

C. Complete the chart.

	Original	Comparative	Superlative
1.	tall		
2.	beautiful		
3.			smallest
4.		more colourful	
5.			freshest
6.	much		
7.		less	
8.			scariest
9.	active		

D. Write one or two sentences using all three forms of an adjective.

_____

_____

_____

Section 2

Grammar

A **noun** can be used to describe another noun in the same way as an **adjective**.

Example

Baby Bobo is our new <u>family</u> member.

E.   Unscramble the words to write what each picture is. Then circle the noun used as an adjective.

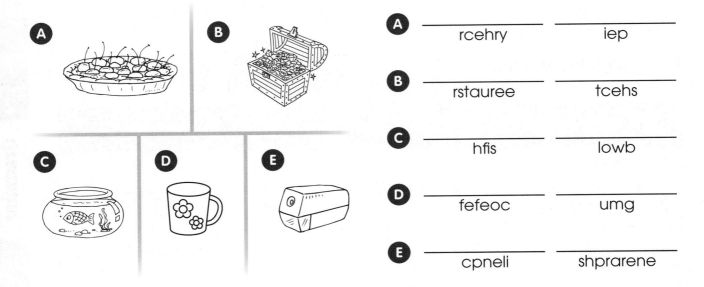

A	rcehry	iep
B	rstauree	tcehs
C	hfis	lowb
D	fefeoc	umg
E	cpneli	shprarene

F.   Fill in the blanks with the correct nouns as adjectives.

> basketball   radio   chocolate
>
> sailing   music

1.   The _____ boat is in the harbour.

2.   She ordered a _____ sundae.

3.   Greg is trying out for the _____ team.

4.   Let's listen to the _____ program.

5.   The instruments are in the _____ room.

G. Complete the sentences using suitable nouns as adjectives.

1. This _____ program is very user-friendly.

2. Let's meet at the _____ court for lunch.

3. My _____ clock is not working.

4. The _____ clips look nice on you.

5. Dad has bought a _____ ring for Mom.

6. Our car is stuck in the _____ jam.

7. My parents held a _____ party for me.

8. Do you want to get an _____ cider?

9. The children are looking at the dolls in the _____ store.

10. I would like to get some _____ candy at the fun fair.

11. Gina is going to write a letter to her _____ pal.

Words that I Have Learned

Adjectives

_____

_____

_____

UNIT

6 Adverbs

An **adverb** is a word that describes a verb. Adverbs explain where, when, how, and how long.

Examples

- The girl took the doll <u>away</u>. ← where
- The Watts go there <u>weekly</u>. ← when
- The dog barked <u>fiercely</u>. ← how
- The snow seemed to fall <u>forever</u>. ← how long

A. Circle the adverbs in the sentences.

1. I will let you have the report later.

2. He had an accident because he drove carelessly.

3. They worked hard to make sure that they could finish the job before noon.

4. The boys usually play hockey at the arena on weekends.

5. Mrs. Watson left for Nova Scotia yesterday.

6. The smart kid solved the problem easily.

7. There is hardly any juice left in the jug.

8. Would you like to come here for lunch?

9. The party went well and they all had a great time.

10. The kids sang wonderfully at the concert.

Most adverbs are formed by adding "ly" to an adjective.

For adjectives ending in "y", drop the "y" and add "ily" to form an adverb.

Examples

- My sister and I are folding the clothes <u>neatly</u>.
- The children were singing <u>happily</u>.

B. **Change the adjectives to adverbs and fill in the blanks.**

> thoughtful   patient   special
>
> quick   sudden   easy   serious
>
> cautious   awful   solemn

1. The pirate asked his man to row _____ .

2. The lights went off _____ .

3. It is _____ smelly here.

4. They entered the dark cave _____ .

5. He is thinking _____ about the riddle.

6. They are waiting for their coach _____ .

7. Do you think you can pass the test _____ ?

8. The soldiers are standing _____ at the entrance.

9. They planned their trip _____ .

10. This dress is _____ designed for you.

A **comparative adverb** compares two actions. For adverbs ending in "ly", use "more" before the adverb. For adverbs that have the same form as their adjective counterparts, add "er". Some adverbs have two comparative forms; some are irregular and have different words for their comparative forms.

Examples

- gently ⟶ more gently
- fast ⟶ faster
- loud ⟶ louder/
     more loudly
- far ⟶ farther/
     further

C. **Change the adverbs to their comparative forms. Then fill in the blanks with the correct comparative adverbs.**

neatly _____   high _____

well _____   soon _____

sweetly _____   hard _____

1. The robin sings _____ than the blue jay.

2. My friend works _____ than me.

3. Bella jumped _____ than Alyssa in the high jump event last year.

4. Our guests arrived _____ than we expected.

5. Colton has kept his bedroom _____ than his elder sister.

6. Hailey plays the guitar _____ than she plays the piano.

D. Fill in the blanks with the correct comparative adverbs.

1. The sun is shining _____
   brightlier/more brightly
   today than it did yesterday.

2. My mom gets up _____
   earlier/more early
   than me every day.

3. Mila waited _____ for the show to start than
   eagerlier/more eagerly
   everyone else.

4. This dolphin swims _____ to us than the other
   nearer/more nearly
   dolphins.

5. They rowed their boat _____ down the river
   lower/more lowly
   than we did.

6. The children were careful to walk up and down the stairs
   _____ than usual.
   softlier/more softly

Words that I Have Learned

Adverbs

_____

_____

_____

UNIT 7 Prepositions

A **preposition** is a small word that relates a noun or a pronoun with another noun, adjective, or verb. There are different types of prepositions.

A **preposition of place** indicates the location of someone or something.

Examples

- There is a light <u>over</u> the table.
- Something <u>under</u> the carpet is moving!

A. Circle the correct prepositions of place to complete the sentences.

1. The bus stop is right **below / across** the street.

2. There is a flower shop **inside / between** the café and the pet store.

3. Let's take a rest **under / over** the tree.

4. We go to our cottage **by / outside** the lake every summer.

5. The cat hid **on / behind** the bushes.

6. The pepper is placed **beside / inside** the salt.

7. The figurine **in / on** the fireplace mantel was a gift from my best friend.

8. The hot-air balloon **over / below** us is big and colourful.

A **preposition of time** helps indicate when or what time an event takes place.

Examples

- We play <u>during</u> recess.
- Jimmy stayed there <u>until</u> noon.

B.   Fill in the blanks with the correct prepositions of time.

Prepositions of Time

at   in   on   by   during   since   until

1.   Please do not use your cellphone _____ the musical performance.

2.   It has been raining _____ last Monday.

3.   We will gather for the countdown _____ New Year's Eve.

4.   The antique clock strikes 12 times _____ midnight.

5.   The coach will not return _____ five o'clock.   We have lots of time for sightseeing.

6.   Miss Spencer's class will have an outing to a pumpkin patch _____ Friday morning.

7.   Please submit all required documents _____ September 30 or your application will not be considered.

8.   There is little traffic on the highway late _____ the night.

A **preposition of direction** helps indicate where someone or something is going.

Examples

- The old man climbed <u>up</u> the stairs slowly.
- Nova walked <u>toward</u> the notice board.

C. **Circle the preposition of direction in each sentence. Check the box if it is correct. If not, write the correct preposition above it.**

1. The mouse scurried up the hole in the wall.

2. Allison likes strolling along the seashore after dinner.

3. We drove after the service station without stopping.

4. The beautiful island is located one kilometre along the coast.

5. The curious cat chased after the chipmunk.

6. The big snowball rolled up the slope at a high speed.

7. Walking off the dense woods can be dangerous.

8. The koala climbed up the tree where its home was.

9. Willis walked across the street to the arcade.

A **preposition of agent or instrument** indicates that the action is caused by someone or something.

Examples

- This story was written <u>by</u> Catherine.
- Elias likes drawing <u>with</u> crayons.

D. Circle the correct prepositions and add your own words to complete the sentences.

1. I usually go to the library **by / with** _____ .

2. Mom opened the canned soup **by / with** _____ .

3. The masterpiece was painted **by / with** _____ .

4. Ryan mixed the ingredients **by / with** _____ .

5. Cora will send me the parcel **by / with** _____ .

6. Don't kick the chair **by / with** _____ .

7. You have to log in **by / with** _____ .

Words that I Have Learned

Prepositions of...

Place _____

Time _____

Direction _____

Agent or Instrument _____

UNIT

8 Conjunctions

A **conjunction** is a joining word. It is used to join a word to another word, or a sentence to another sentence.

Examples

- Matt likes Popsicles <u>and</u> ice cream.
- You may have an ice cream <u>or</u> a Popsicle <u>but</u> not both.
- We are leaving for Calgary <u>but</u> Dad has to stay behind.

A.   Circle the correct conjunctions to complete the sentences.

1.   The Fall Fair has many displays **and / or** thrilling rides.

2.   Most of the children wanted an outing **and / but** Mrs. Baker suggested a pizza party instead.

3.   Was he born on the eighth **or / but** the eighteenth of May?

4.   They bought juice, vegetables, fruits, **but / and** bread.

5.   Both Cindy **and / or** Wilfred represent our class.

6.   Which painting is yours, this one **or / but** that one?

7.   He wants to be a professional baseball player **but / and** he is not good at batting **and / or** pitching.

8.   I cannot do math **and / but** watch TV at the same time.

9.   The pumpkin is bright orange **or / and** weighs more than 200 kilograms.

B. Combine each pair of sentences into one sentence using "and", "or", or "but".

1. The pony eats oats.
   The pony eats hay.

   _____

   _____

2. Owls sleep during the day and hunt at night. Bats sleep during the day and hunt at night.

   _____

   _____

3. The days are hot in the summer. The days are cold in the winter.

   _____

   _____

4. We can take the midnight flight. We can take the morning flight the next day.

   _____

   _____

5. Greg does not like to eat spinach. Greg likes to eat broccoli.

   _____

   _____

6. You can go there to apply in person. You can fill in the form online.

   _____

   _____

"**Before**" and "**after**" link sentences together as **conjunctions**. They can be used to begin or placed in the middle of a sentence. Note that when "before" or "after" is used to begin a sentence, a comma is needed between the clauses.

Examples

I packed my clothes. Then I went swimming.

- <u>Before</u> I went swimming, I packed my clothes.

- I went swimming <u>after</u> I packed my clothes.

C. Circle the conjunction in each sentence. Check the box if it is correct. If not, write the correct conjunction above it.

1. Everyone has to wear the seat belt before getting into the car. ☐

2. I always put the toys back in the box after I finish playing. ☐

3. After you go to bed, set the alarm clock. ☐

4. We helped Mom clean up before the guests left. ☐

5. Give it to the librarian after you fill out the form. ☐

6. Before we got on the bus, we showed the transfer tickets to the bus driver. ☐

7. After Emma has touched up the photos, she will send them to me. ☐

8. We had to go through security check after we went on board. ☐

Security Check

D.   Read the recipe. Then answer the questions with "before" or "after".

Rice Krispy Treats

6 cups Rice Krispies
200 grams butter
4 cups marshmallows
1 cup peanut butter

- Melt butter, marshmallows, and peanut butter over low heat in a large pan.
- Remove from heat and stir in Rice Krispies.
- Spread into a large buttered flat pan.
- Pat down with buttered hands.
- Cool and cut into squares.

1. When should you remove the pan from the heat?

   _____

2. When should you stir in the Rice Krispies?

   _____

3. When should you butter your hands?

   _____

Words that I Have Learned

Conjunctions

   _____

   _____

   _____

Section
2

Grammar

UNIT

9 The Sentence: Subject and Predicate

Examples

A sentence contains a subject and a predicate. The **subject** of a sentence tells whom or what the sentence is about. It can be a noun or a pronoun.

A **compound subject** has two or more nouns or pronouns. They are joined by the conjunction "and".

- <u>My brother</u> is a teacher. <u>He</u> teaches music.

- <u>Brad and I</u> slept in the same tent.

A. **Underline the subjects. Then write them in the correct boxes.**

The subject of a sentence may consist of a noun and other words that modify it, such as articles and adjectives.

Last week, Rita and I went to summer camp. We joined many activities such as swimming, ball games, and talent shows. My favourite activity was arts and crafts. Hats, beaded bracelets, and dreamcatchers were some of the things we made. After the camp, I gave a bracelet to my mom. The bracelet has colourful beads. Mom likes it very much. She wears it all the time.

Subject		Compound Subject
Noun	**Pronoun**	

The **predicate** of a sentence is the part that describes the subject. It contains a verb describing the action performed by the subject.

Steven <u>sings very well</u>.

B. **Look at the picture. Match the subjects with the correct predicates. Write the letters.**

1. The zoo _____

2. The zookeeper _____

3. The elephant _____

4. The panda _____

5. The tiger _____

6. Josh _____

7. Edith and I _____

A. loves the hay.

B. is covered in stripes.

C. is a lot of fun!

D. is in the tree!

E. are looking at the animals.

F. is feeding the elephant.

G. eats bamboo leaves.

C. **Circle the subjects and underline the predicates of the sentences. Then change all subjects to compound subjects by writing above the circled words.**

My parents and I

1. (I) <u>like going shopping</u>.

2. Jill went to the store.

3. Charlie wanted to have pizza for lunch.

4. My mom took me to the beach.

5. His pet dog slept on the couch in the living room.

6. Cookies are Jamie's favourite snacks to eat.

7. The ducks on the farm became friends.

8. The noisy girls talked and talked during the movie.

9. The big frog swallowed the flies around it.

10. Watermelons are too sweet for both Grandpa and Grandma.

11. You are my best friend in the whole world.

12. The robots in the toy box over there belong to Kayla.

D. Complete the sentences.

Add Subjects

1. _____ made a huge mess.

2. _____ worked on the project together.

3. _____ found a secret passage.

4. _____ climbed the tallest tree.

5. _____ are important to plants.

Add Predicates

1.  The superhero _____ .

2.  My aunt and uncle _____ .

3.  Lions and tigers _____ .

4.  Strawberry milkshakes _____ .

5.  We _____ .

Words that I Have Learned

_____

_____

_____

UNIT 10 Subject-verb Agreement

In a sentence, the **verb** must **agree** with the **subject**. If the subject is singular, a singular verb should be used. If the subject is plural, a plural verb should be used.

Examples

- <u>Vincent is</u> a fast runner.
- <u>The players are</u> tired.

A. Underline the subject and circle the verb in each sentence. Then write "S" on the line if the subject and the verb are singular, and write "P" if they are plural.

1. The squirrel has eaten our cherries. _____

2. The hunting dog is well trained. _____

3. The children were swimming in the pool. _____

4. This rabbit always hides behind the bushes. _____

5. Those potatoes were taken from Grandpa's farm. _____

6. These sheep have their wool shorn by the farmer. _____

7. The penguins like to swim in the ocean. _____

8. The sun is shining brightly in the sky. _____

9. One of the eggs in the carton is cracked. _____

10. The porcelain dolls were very expensive and delicate. _____

B. **Fill in the blanks with the correct verb forms.**

1. | prepare |
   |---|
   | prepares |

   Each of us _____ one item for the party.

2. | is |
   |---|
   | are |

   How much _____ this DVD?

3. | am |
   |---|
   | are |

   Isla and I _____ twin sisters.

4. | jump |
   |---|
   | jumps |

   He always _____ in leaves.

5. | walk |
   |---|
   | walks |

   Jay and Olivia _____ to school.

6. | has |
   |---|
   | have |

   The tallest tree in the woods _____ magic.

7. | was |
   |---|
   | were |

   There _____ a lot of mistakes in his writing.

C. **Check the box if there is subject-verb agreement in each sentence. If not, cross out the verb and write above it.**

1. We is picking strawberries. ☐

2. The girls plays soccer together. ☐

3. The flowers are in full bloom. ☐

4. I am going to check the mail. ☐

5. Are James working on the assignment? ☐

6. Everyone have come to celebrate with us. ☐

D.   Fill in the blanks with the correct forms of the verbs.

Fred _____ (play) the piano very well.   His

parents _____ (be) very proud of him. They

_____ (do) not watch TV when he plays

the piano. His piano _____ (be)

very expensive. It _____ (be)

a present from his parents. He

_____ (do) not let others

play it. He _____ (practise) every

day after school.

It _____ (be) my birthday last Friday. Mom and

Dad bought me a dog. He _____ (be) very cute. I

_____ (call) him Kiki. He _____ (have)

big ears. They _____ (stick) out when I call

his name. I _____ (like) playing with him.

I think he _____ (enjoy) playing with

me too. Kiki and I _____ (be) going

to be best friends forever. We _____

(love) each other.

E. Complete the sentences.

Decide whether the subjects are singular or plural first.

1. The cow and the sheep _____

   _____ .

2. Miss Clark _____

   _____ .

3. All the girls in my class _____

   _____ .

4. My friends and I _____

   _____ .

5. The smoothie _____

   _____ .

6. Everyone _____

   _____ .

7. The good news _____

   _____ .

Words that I Have Learned

_____

_____

_____

UNIT 11 Simple, Compound, and Complex Sentences

A **simple sentence** expresses a complete thought. It is made up of a subject and a predicate.

Examples

• A man is beside a car. (sentence)
• A man and a car (not a sentence)

A. Write "S" in the circle if each group of words is a sentence. Write "N" if it is not a sentence.

1. We enjoy sunbathing.   ◯

2. The morning sun is soothing.   ◯

3. The cool pool water.   ◯

4. My lazy poodle.   ◯

5. I swim with my cousins.   ◯

B. Draw lines to match the subjects with the predicates to form simple sentences.

Subject	Predicate

1. The leaves   •   • crawls slowly.

2. The smart child •   • rattled loudly.

3. The machine   •   • change colour in the fall.

4. Our trip   •   • likes chewing shoes.

5. The snail   •   • solved the puzzle very soon.

6. Kate's puppy   •   • was cancelled because of the bad weather.

A **compound sentence** is made up of two simple sentences joined together by a conjunction (and/or/but).

Examples

- The film was funny. We laughed aloud. (simple sentences)
- The film was funny and we laughed aloud. (compound sentence)

C. **Form a compound sentence by joining each pair of simple sentences with the correct conjunction.**

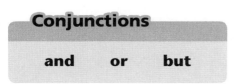

Conjunctions

| and | or | but |

1. My computer is old. It still works.

   _____

2. The beach is beautiful. It is easy to get to.

   _____

3. I will join the party. I have to leave early.

   _____

4. My brother is little. He needs to take an afternoon nap.

   _____

5. We will watch the football game. We will go out for dinner.

   _____

6. Becky needs to study. She has soccer practice.

   _____

7. We can have pizza at home. We can eat out.

   _____

A **complex sentence** is a sentence that includes one independent clause, at least one dependent clause, and a subordinating conjunction, which joins the independent clause and the dependent clause together.

An **independent clause** is a complete sentence that can stand on its own.

A **dependent clause** is an incomplete sentence that cannot stand on its own.

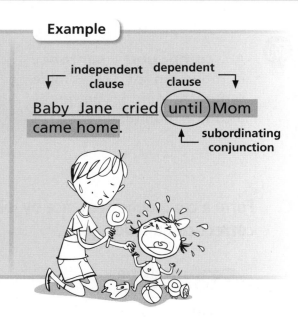

Example

independent clause   dependent clause

Baby Jane cried (until) Mom came home.

subordinating conjunction

D. **For each sentence, underline the independent clause and put parentheses around the dependent clause. Then circle the subordinating conjunction.**

1. The meeting will be postponed if fewer than five members show up.

2. Let's meet at the entrance before the game starts.

3. Sophia called Nicole while she was waiting for the bus.

4. When we arrived in the city, we checked into the hotel first.

5. Tyler never stops practising unless he is sick.

6. Although the event is over, everyone is still very excited.

7. The family stayed on the farm until the sun set.

8. The children play in puddles whenever it rains.

E. Use the correct subordinating conjunctions to join the clauses to form complex sentences.

Subordinating Conjunctions

after   although   while   since

1. I tried to keep calm. I was really scared.

   _____

   _____

2. Handle it with great care. This is the last egg we have.

   _____

   _____

3. Randy finished eating his pasta. He would like some desserts.

   _____

   _____

4. Mom played with me in the park. Dad went to pick up my brother.

   _____

   _____

Words that I Have Learned

_____

_____

_____

UNIT 12 Phrases and Clauses

A **phrase** is a group of words in a sentence that does not include a subject and a verb.

A **clause** is a group of words that has the same structure as a sentence but is part of a larger sentence. Clauses are linked together by a conjunction to form a sentence.

Examples

- Let's have dinner <u>at the restaurant over there</u>. (phrase)
- <u>I joined this program</u> because <u>I like swimming</u>. (clauses)

A. **Check the correct boxes to show whether the underlined words are phrases or clauses.**

1. <u>He has always wanted to be a firefighter</u> since he was seven.

2. <u>To win the game</u>, you need to get all the sticks.

3. <u>My hair sticks out</u> when I hear a squeaky voice.

4. We turned off the lights <u>at the beginning of the party</u>.

5. Even if it rains, <u>Mr. Franco will go jogging all the same</u>.

6. I tried to call you but <u>the line was busy</u>.

7. <u>Because of the stormy weather last night</u>, the concert was cancelled.

8. She makes it disappear <u>with her magic wand</u>.

	1	2	3	4	5	6	7	8
Phrase								
Clause								

B. **Underline the phrases in the sentences.**

1. The little polar bear always climbs on its mother's back.

2. Gilbert did his best in the performance.

3. Joshua is such a helpful person that he drove us home.

4. Do not call me; I will be doing my homework.

5. The flight tickets are expensive during the peak season.

C. **Match the clauses to form sentences. Write the letters. Then circle the conjunctions.**

> **A** we could finish the project   **B** take my orange juice
>
> **C** it looks like new   **D** our car broke down
>
> **E** you go sailing   **F** I came last

1. We worked overnight so _____ .

2. I finished the race although _____ .

3. We are late because _____ .

4. Always wear a life jacket when _____ .

5. If you don't have milk, _____ .

6. Dad has polished the car and _____ .

A **noun phrase** is any phrase that includes a noun and all its modifiers.

Example

We had to drive through <u>a long winding road</u> to get to <u>the campsite</u>.

D. Form noun phrases with the given words to complete the sentences.

1. _____ made me fall asleep.

2. They really enjoy _____ _____ .

3. Mom was shocked by _____ _____ .

4. Mr. Davis has _____ for _____ .

5. _____ were impressed by _____ .

6. _____ in _____ are driving people away.

7. _____ lined up for _____ .

8. _____ earned _____ from _____ .

1.	boring movie this
2.	dishes our mouth-watering
3.	creature the fluffy
4.	great sympathy; blind the
5.	of us all; cellphone the state-of-the-art
6.	appalling the conditions living; area this
7.	people of hundreds; turkeys free
8.	monkey's the performance; lot of a applause; audience the

A **prepositional phrase** begins with a preposition and includes a noun or a pronoun. It can describe a noun as an adjective phrase. It can also describe a verb as an adverb phrase.

Examples

- The doll <u>in the smaller box</u> is for Janet.   adjective phrase
- I decorate the box <u>with paper flowers</u>.   adverb phrase

E. **Match the groups of words with the correct prepositional phrases to form sentences. Write the letters.**

1. Mrs. Francisco takes care of us ____ .

2. Our cat is the one ____ .

3. Please write your name ____ .

4. John was first in the race ____ .

5. I want the clock in the shape ____ .

(A) on the first page

(B) of a frog

(C) at the beginning

(D) with a short tail

(E) at mealtime

F. **Write sentences using phrases with the given prepositions.**

Adjective Phrase

in _____

at _____

Adverb Phrase

for _____

with _____

Words that I Have Learned

_____

_____

_____

UNIT

13 More on Phrases

A **verb phrase** functions in the same way as a single verb in a sentence.

Examples

- The wind <u>blows</u> hard. ← verb
- The wind <u>is blowing</u> hard. ← verb phrase

A. Read each sentence. Check the box if there is a verb phrase in the sentence and then circle it. If not, put a cross in the box.

Verb Phrase

1. I wish I could ride a real horse.

2. They should have tidied up their rooms.

3. We had a barbecue lunch yesterday.

4. You should keep an eye on your luggage.

5. Uncle Ben is working hard on his construction project.

6. The Wellings flew to Vancouver last Sunday.

B. Fill in the blanks with verb phrases using the given verbs.

> try   meet   watch   run   visit   rain

1. We had better wait here. It _____ heavily.

2. They _____ us next Sunday.

3. The robbers _____ away when I saw them.

4. We _____ each other before.

5. You would have won if you _____ your best.

6. Shh! I _____ the news.

A **verbal phrase** begins with the "ing" form of a verb and functions as a noun.

Example

Gina likes <u>collecting necklaces</u>.

C. **Underline the verbal phrases and circle the verb phrases in the sentences.**

1. Gosh! The TV is not working.

2. I spend a lot of time working out every day.

3. Flying kites is their favourite summer activity.

4. Jumping into the pool is what I want to do most.

5. The police have been looking into the case for months.

6. I will never forget walking up the stairs to the top of the cathedral.

D. **Complete the sentences with verbal phrases using the given words.**

1. Glen plays ball with his friends every day. He is good at _____ (catch the ball).

2. Julianna sings in the choir. She loves _____ (sing loudly) when she is alone.

3. Stop _____ (make that noise). It's annoying!

4. _____ (write a novel) is what Elias is currently doing.

5. _____ (eat more vegetables) is good for your health.

An **adjective phrase** functions in the same way as a single adjective. It is used to describe a noun. It may or may not have an adjective in itself.

Examples

- The man <u>with a beard</u> is Mr. Phil.
- He is <u>very kind</u>.

E. Underline the adjective phrase in each sentence. Then circle the adjective if it has one.

1. The dog in the kennel barked loudly.

2. Keith was pretty sure that was his watch.

3. The seats on the bus were all occupied.

4. Mom likes the dress with the flower patterns best.

5. The magic show was very impressive.

F. Write sentences using the given nouns and adjective phrases.

1. movie / terribly scary

   _____

2. book / with a hard cover

   _____

3. idea / totally outrageous

   _____

4. baby koala / on its mother's back

   _____

An **adverb phrase** functions in the same way as a single adverb. It is used to describe a verb.

Examples

Mom let the pie sit <u>for an hour</u>. Then she put it <u>in the fridge</u>.

G.   Unscramble the adverb phrases to complete the sentences.

Yesterday, there was a basketball match

1._____ . It was between our

school team and Island School's team.

My classmates and I made some signs

2._____ . We waved them

3._____ in the air whenever our

team made a shot. Both teams played

4._____ . Unfortunately, our team

lost by three points 5._____ .

1. our for team

2. school after

3. up high

4. hard really

5. the in end

H.   Write sentences using these adverb phrases.

1. near the lake   _____

2. next Saturday   _____

3. every summer   _____

Words that I Have Learned

_____

_____

_____

Section
2

Grammar

UNIT

14 Punctuation

Quotation marks are used in pairs. They can be used to:

- contain the exact words of a speaker or from a book.

- indicate the titles of songs, books, movies, newspapers, etc.

Examples

- "No fighting," Miss Dolly said.

- Don't you remember the famous line: "A rose by any other name will smell as sweet"?

- Do you know the song "A Whole New World"?

A. Check the boxes if the quotation marks are used correctly in the sentences. If not, cross them out and add quotation marks at the correct places.

Correct Quotation Marks

1. The movie Lord of the Rings "won many Oscars". ☐

2. Have you read the book "Cat in the Hat"? ☐

3. Beauty and the Beast is on at the "Princess of Wales Theatre". ☐

4. "Mom always watches" The Basic Chef for new recipes. ☐

5. Finding Nemo is a "popular movie". ☐

6. We can call it "Project X". ☐

7. "Jamie asked", Where are the keys? ☐

B. Add quotation marks where necessary.

1. Good morning class, said Mrs. Axford.

2. Thank you for shopping with us, said the salesperson.

3. Mary shouted, See you later and have a wonderful day!

A **semicolon** replaces a conjunction to join two related sentences.

I felt sleepy and I fell asleep quickly.

I felt sleepy; I fell asleep quickly.

C. Rewrite the sentences by replacing the conjunctions with semicolons.

1. Tim is a fast runner and he has won many medals.

   _____

   _____

2. This story is very interesting so I have read it many times.

   _____

   _____

3. Tomorrow is the last day of school so we need to clear out our lockers.

   _____

   _____

4. My brother is crazy about SpongeBob and he has T-shirts with the character on them.

   _____

   _____

5. We are going to the pet store as I want to look at the puppies.

   _____

   _____

Apostrophes are used to show possession or to make contractions.

Possession is shown by using an apostrophe and the letter "s". For plural nouns that already end with "s", just add an apostrophe at the end to show possession.

A contraction is a single word that is formed by combining and shortening two words. An apostrophe is used to replace letters.

Examples

Showing possession:

- This is Benjamin's jacket.
- Is this the girls' washroom?

Making contractions:

- they are ⟶ they're
- will not ⟶ won't

D. **Tell whether the apostrophe in each sentence is showing possession or making a contraction. Write the letter in the correct box.**

A Strawberry is my uncle's favourite ice cream flavour.

B Who's coming to the restaurant?

C She's read the book before.

D Spencer is Magnus's best friend.

E Janice's cat is sleeping in the yard.

F They don't want to go to the movies.

G You shouldn't shout in the library.

Showing Possession

Making a Contraction

E. **Circle the correct words to show possession.**

1. This hat belongs to Jordan. This is **Jordans' / Jordan's** hat.

2. Those candies belong to James. They are **Jame's / James's** candies.

3. These expensive instruments belong to the musicians. They are the **musician's / musicians'** instruments.

4. This book belongs to Suzy. It has **Suzy's / Suzies'** name on it.

F. Write the contractions of the given words.

1. _____
   where is

2. _____
   I am

3. _____
   does not

4. _____
   would not

5. _____
   there is

6. _____
   are not

7. _____
   you are

8. _____
   cannot

9. _____
   is not

10. _____
   must not

11. _____
   should not

12. _____
   she will

Don't forget the apostrophe.

don **,** t

do not

G. Write sentences with the contractions of the given words.

A **they are**   **B** **let us**   **C** **did not**   **D** **how is**

A _____

B _____

C _____

D _____

Words that I Have Learned

_____

_____

_____

A. Circle the answers.

1. Which sentence has the subject of a verb underlined?

   I <u>read</u> a book.

   Sheila dances <u>salsa</u>.

   <u>Russia</u> is a large country.

2. Which sentence has the direct object of a verb underlined?

   My cat eats <u>fish</u>.

   <u>My dream</u> was scary.

   Jonah <u>scared</u> Tommy.

3. Which sentence has the indirect object of a verb underlined?

   My mom gives <u>me</u> a ring.

   Sal buys <u>new</u> shoes.

   You hear her <u>screams</u>.

4. Which pronoun is correct in the sentence below?

   _____ named her Eve.

   Them

   Us

   They

5. Which is the comparative adjective of "fresh"?

   freshest

   freshier

   fresher

6. Which is the superlative adjective of "nervous"?

   nervouser

   most nervous

   more nervous

7. Which adverb form is correct in the sentence below?

   She dances _____ than her rival.

   gracefully

   more gracefully

   most gracefully

8. Which conjunction is correct in the sentence below?

   The baby cried _____ it was fed.

   since

   until

   during

9. Which preposition of direction is correct in the sentence below?

The car swerves _____ the fence.

off

up

toward

10. Which is not a preposition of agent or instrument?

with

along

by

11. Which can be the predicate of a sentence?

Corey and I

the loud music

ran all the way home

12. Which shows correct subject-verb agreement?

He wake up in the morning.

Kelly sings in the shower.

We was in the park.

13. Which is a simple sentence?

I am funny and I am great.

The breeze is cool.

Although he begged and pleaded, I did not forgive him.

14. Which sentence has a verbal phrase underlined?

I love <u>swimming in the morning</u>.

<u>My mom</u> is working all night.

John <u>will build</u> a tree house.

15. Which sentence has an adverb phrase underlined?

Donna walks to school <u>every day</u>.

Bill jumps higher <u>than Will</u>.

I can buy <u>two dresses</u>.

16. Which sentence uses the semicolon correctly?

I woke up too early; and I slept late.

I woke up too early; I am sleepy.

I woke up; early.

Subject-verb Agreement and Verb Tenses

B.   Circle the correct words to show subject-verb agreement.

Hop and Scotch **live / lives** in the forest. They discovered a garden outside the forest. It **belong / belongs** to a farmer called Mr. Gregory. Sometimes, the rabbits go there to munch on the delicious vegetables.

It is morning and Hop and Scotch **has / have** just woken up. Scotch **say / says** , "Let's go to the garden and eat some vegetables." "I **like / likes** your idea," replies Hop.

Scotch is a very competitive rabbit. "I think we should have a race," he says. Hop is not competitive but he thinks this could make it a fun trip. "Sure!" Hop **agree / agrees** . And off they **go / goes** !

C.   Write the verbs in the correct verb tense.

1. Mr. Gregory _____ (enjoy) working in his garden.

2. Hop and Scotch _____ (eat) some carrots and radishes from the garden last week.

3. Scotch _____ (run) very fast to get ahead of Hop.

4. Hop _____ (expect) to find plenty of delicious vegetables in the garden later.

5. The scarecrow in the garden _____ (scare) them the other night when they _____ (try) to steal some food.

6. The two rabbits _____ (laugh) as they race each other.

Common Nouns, Proper Nouns, and Pronouns

D. Circle the common nouns in red and the proper nouns in blue. Then underline the pronouns.

Before the rabbits have gone very far, they meet Buzzer, a bumblebee, and Flutter, a robin. "Move it, you two!" says Scotch. "We are in the middle of a race to Mr. Gregory's garden!"

"We are sorry to bother you but we need help," says Buzzer. "I cannot find flowers and I need nectar for my family. And Flutter needs help finding worms to eat."

"That's not our problem. It's yours. Good luck!" says Scotch before he hops away.

"I will help you both," says Hop. Together, they are able to find some flowers and worms.

Subjects and Predicates

E. Complete each sentence by adding a subject or a predicate.

1. _____ are racing to Mr. Gregory's garden.

2. _____ was having a difficult time finding worms.

3. Mr. Gregory's garden _____ .

4. Hop and Scotch _____ .

5. Buzzer and Flutter _____ .

Simple, Compound, and Complex Sentences

F.   Read the story. Identify the type of each sentence by putting the number in the correct box.

1 When they arrive at the garden, Flutter, Buzzer, and Hop are surprised to see that Scotch has eaten all the vegetables. **2** Hop is disappointed in Scotch and he is sad that he did not get to enjoy any of the vegetables.

3 Scotch apologizes to Hop. **4** He says he won the race and he deserves to eat everything. **5** Hop agrees with Scotch but he did not expect Scotch to leave him with nothing.

6 Although Hop wanted some vegetables, he knows there are other things to eat in the forest. **7** When he turns to his friends, Buzzer and Flutter tell him that they have an idea. **8** Buzzer tells him about another vegetable garden. **9** It is even better.

Simple Sentence	Compound Sentence	Complex Sentence

Phrases and Clauses

G.   Write to show whether the underlined words are a phrase "P" or a clause "C".

1. <u>Hop was excited to eat some vegetables</u> from Mr. Gregory's garden.   ◯

2. <u>Scotch ate all the vegetables</u> and left none for Hop.   ◯

3. Buzzer and Flutter show Hop <u>another vegetable garden</u>.   ◯

4. They want to return <u>the kindness Hop has shown them</u>.   ◯

H. Write "N" for noun phrases, "P" for prepositional phrases, "V" for verb phrases, "ADJ" for adjective phrases, and "ADV" for adverb phrases.

1. <u>The yummy cabbage</u> is Scotch's favourite. ◯

2. The vegetables <u>in the garden</u> are all gone. ◯

3. Mr. Gregory <u>does not know</u> who ate the vegetables. ◯

4. Buzzer and Flutter lead Hop <u>to the other garden</u>. ◯

5. Hop talks <u>very excitedly</u> with his new friends, Buzzer and Flutter. ◯

Conjunctions and Punctuation

I. Fill in the blanks with the correct conjunctions and put the correct punctuation marks in the circles.

The three friends arrive at the new garden _____ they are overjoyed. Not only is there a lot of vegetables _____ there are many different kinds as well. Hop eats a little of everything. "I ◯ ll have some lettuce _____ some cabbage!" he says. ◯ Look, Buzzer! ◯ says Hop. "There are many flowers here for you!"

"See all these worms, Flutter?" Buzzer says. "You can have them all!"

◯ I ◯ m so happy I didn ◯ t win the race today," Hop admits as he, Buzzer, and Flutter relax in the sunshine _____ their healthful and delicious meal. ◯ Instead I am able to enjoy all of this with my wonderful friends! ◯

Section 3

Vocabulary

UNIT

1 Adaptation Words

behavioural   camouflage   environment
evolutionary   habitat   organism
predator   structural   survive

in summer   in winter

adaptation

Animal Adaptation

Did you know that even in the driest deserts, coldest tundra, and darkest ocean waters live animals, plants, and organisms that are able to survive? They are able to survive and live to reproduce in their harsh environments through adaptation.

Adaptation is an evolutionary change that has developed over many generations to help animals and organisms live successfully in their habitats. The adaptations can be divided into structural and behavioural adaptations.

Camouflage, a structural adaptation, allows animals to blend in with their surroundings. For example, Arctic hares have grey or brown coats in the summer and white coats in the winter months. It helps them camouflage and escape from their predators. The striped tiger, a formidable predator, blends well in the long, tall orange-yellow grasses while stalking its prey.

Behavioural adaptation is the way an animal responds to and interacts with its external environment. In North America, raccoons have changed their habits due to land development that has destroyed their natural habitats. They have learned to use attics, basements, and storage sheds as homes. They raid and open garbage cans with their dexterous fingers for leftovers instead of foraging for food in the forests. They are fast becoming more than just a nuisance!

A. **Unscramble the adaptation words with the help of the definitions. Then fill in the blanks with the correct words.**

Adaptation Word	Definition

_____ : relating to behaviour
vuoihbealar

_____ : relating to gradual development
ratyluoniveo

_____ : single-cell life forms
omssgarin

_____ : surroundings
nornemevint

_____ : continue to live
ruevvis

_____ : disguise, blend in
aeaflgmocu

1. Animals are able to _____ in harsh environments.

2. Adaptation helps animals, plants, and _____ survive in harsh climates.

3. Adaptation is an _____ change that has developed over time.

4. There are two types of adaptations: structural and _____ .

5. An example of a structural adaptation is _____ .

6. Behavioural adaptation occurs when an animal responds to and interacts with the natural _____ .

B. Read the descriptions of each animal's habitat and adaptational changes. Then write the correct animal name.

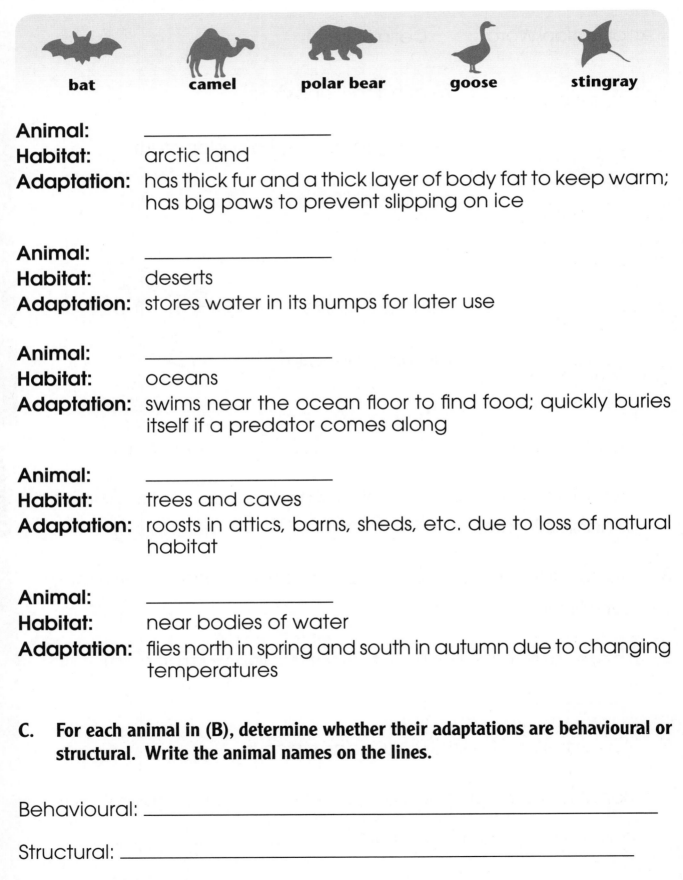

bat   camel   polar bear   goose   stingray

Animal: _____

Habitat: arctic land

Adaptation: has thick fur and a thick layer of body fat to keep warm; has big paws to prevent slipping on ice

Animal: _____

Habitat: deserts

Adaptation: stores water in its humps for later use

Animal: _____

Habitat: oceans

Adaptation: swims near the ocean floor to find food; quickly buries itself if a predator comes along

Animal: _____

Habitat: trees and caves

Adaptation: roosts in attics, barns, sheds, etc. due to loss of natural habitat

Animal: _____

Habitat: near bodies of water

Adaptation: flies north in spring and south in autumn due to changing temperatures

C. For each animal in (B), determine whether their adaptations are behavioural or structural. Write the animal names on the lines.

Behavioural: _____

Structural: _____

D. Make sentences with the adaptation words.

1. adaptation _____

_____

2. predator _____

_____

3. habitat _____

_____

4. survive _____

_____

5. camouflage _____

_____

6. evolutionary _____

_____

Words that I Have Learned

Adaptation Words

_____

_____

_____

_____

Medical Words

congenital   defence   disinfected   doctor
drug   infection   operation   patient   precaution
rejection   sterilized   survive   transplant

hospital

The First Heart Transplant

In December 1967, in Groote Schuur Hospital in Cape Town, South Africa, medical history was made. Dr. Christiaan Barnard performed the first successful transplant of a human heart. The patient, Louis Washkansky, received the heart of a young woman killed in a car accident.

The transplant itself was traumatic, and so were the hours immediately after the operation. There were two main concerns: the problem of possible infection and the possibility that Washkansky's body would reject the new heart. To avoid rejection, doctors gave Washkansky drugs to lessen his body's natural defence so that rejection was less likely. However, with defence weakened, the chance for infection increased. As a precaution, the doctors made sure that everything near Washkansky was sterilized or disinfected.

The transplant was going very well for the first two weeks. Suddenly, a dark spot appeared on one of Washkansky's lungs. Dr. Barnard and his staff did everything possible to save Washkansky, but on the nineteenth day after the operation, Washkansky died.

Although Washkansky did not survive the transplant, the operation was considered a success. It paved the way for many more attempts to follow. Today, heart transplants are performed regularly. Many of those who were born with congenital heart conditions and doomed to die at an early age now live long and healthy lives, thanks to the pioneering efforts of Dr. Christiaan Barnard.

A. **Draw lines to match the medical words with the definitions.**

Medical Word

Definition

1. transplant •

2. drug •

3. doctor •

4. hospital •

5. sterilized •

6. patient •

7. infection •

8. operation •

• a person who practises medicine

• made completely clean and free from bacteria

• caused by germs or bacteria

• a substance used to cure or heal

• a surgical procedure

• replacing a body organ by surgery

• a person receiving medical treatment

• a place where sick people go for care or help

B. **Cross out the word that does not belong in each group. Then explain how the remaining words are related.**

1. transplant   operation   body   surgery

_____

2. human   brain   heart   lungs

_____

3. sterilize   disinfect   precaution   sanitize

_____

4. **doctor**   **nurse**   **lawyer**   **surgeon**

_____

C. **Read the clues and complete the crossword puzzle with the medical words from the passage.**

Across

Ⓐ Dr. Barnard performed the first heart _____ .

Ⓑ A dark spot appeared on one of the patient's _____ .

Ⓒ The patient received a new _____ .

Ⓓ The doctors used drugs to try to avoid _____ .

Down

❶ Everything was sterilized to avoid possible _____ .

❷ Unfortunately, the patient did not _____ .

❸ The _____ was considered a success.

❹ Heart transplants can save the lives of people with _____ heart conditions.

D. **Put the words in order to form sentences. Then circle the medical words in the sentences.**

Some sentences have more than one medical word!

1. doctor / the / healed / the / patient

   _____

2. ambulance / to / rushed / the / hospital / the

   _____

3. successful / heart / the / transplant / was

   _____

4. surgeon / the / is / performing / operation / an

   _____

5. wound / the / prevent / to / sterilized / infection / was

   _____

6. man / the / healthy / drug / made / again / the / taking

   _____

Words that I Have Learned

Medical Words

_____

_____

_____

_____

Herbal Medicine Words

aloe vera   boswellia   cinchona   dandelion
foxglove   ginseng   jojoba   licorice
peppermint   rosemary   sunflower   turmeric

herbal medicine

Plants – Nature's Medicine

Ancient civilizations discovered through experimentation that certain plants contained remedies to illness. They also discovered that some plants contained poisons that were often fatal. Once discovered, plants that were medicinal were cultivated in special gardens. This was the origin of <u>herbal medicine</u> as we know it today.

There are a number of plants that produce medicines. One of the most popular natural medicines in wide use today is ginseng, an ancient Chinese herbal <u>remedy</u> that dates back 5000 years. The leaves of the foxglove plant produce digitalis, which is used to treat heart conditions. It helps the heart beat slower and more regularly. The bark of the South American cinchona tree gives us quinine used to <u>treat</u> malaria. Quinine is also used to make tonic water.

Some herbal plants, such as turmeric, boswellia, and licorice, have anti-inflammatory properties. They work by decreasing the activity of pro-inflammatory cells to help control stiffness, irritation, and pain. Rosemary, another herbal plant, is being studied for its potential in reducing the risk of Alzheimer's disease. Its antibacterial and anti-fungal oil improves blood circulation in the brain and thus helps prevent memory loss. Among household plants, sunflowers can be used to treat various types of colds and coughs, and peppermint can <u>soothe</u> headaches, skin irritations, nausea, and pain, among other ailments. Even dandelions, which are pulled out as weeds, can help treat eczema, arthritis, and an upset stomach.

Some plants are used for topical treatments. The term "topical" refers to the use on the outside of the body, typically on the skin. Two of the most popular plants are aloe vera and jojoba. The creams produced from these plants are sold at cosmetic counters all over the world. They are believed to reduce dryness and skin damage from sunburn.

Like our ancient ancestors, we are discovering the <u>benefits</u> of natural medicines in our everyday life. Creams, herbal teas, and food additives are some of the common uses of plant medicines today.

A. **Complete the chart with the correct herbal medicine words.**

Herbal Medicine Uses

1. _____
   - treat various types of colds and coughs

2. _____
   - help treat eczema, arthritis, and an upset stomach

3. _____
   - reduce dryness of the skin and skin damage from sunburn

4. _____
   - soothes headaches, skin irritations, nausea, and pain

5. _____
   - treat heart conditions
   - help the heart beat slower and more regularly

6. _____
   - treats malaria
   - makes tonic water

7. _____
   - reduces the risk of Alzheimer's disease
   - improves blood circulation in the brain and helps prevent memory loss

8. _____
   - decrease the activity of pro-inflammatory cells to help control stiffness, irritation, and pain

B. Fill in the blanks with the correct herbal medicine words.

Many plants produce 1._____ . One of the most

common natural medicines is 2._____ , an ancient

Chinese herbal remedy. 3._____ , produced from the

leaves of the 4._____ , is used to treat heart conditions.

5._____ from the South American cinchona tree is used to

treat malaria. Other plants like the turmeric have 6._____

properties. There are also plants that are used for 7._____

treatments, like 8._____ and aloe vera.

C. Use context clues to determine the definitions of the underlined words from the passage.

1. herbal medicine

   _____

   _____

2. remedy

   _____

3. treat

   _____

4. soothe

   _____

5. benefits

   _____

D. Identify the medicinal plants.

1.

a _____

2.

g _____

3.

d _____

4.

t _____

5.

p _____

6.

f _____

Words that I Have Learned

Herbal Medicine Words

_____

_____

_____

_____

Section
3
Vocabulary

UNIT 4 **Brain Words**

cerebellum   cerebrum   emotion   function
hypothalamus   identity   medulla oblongata
memory   nervous system   organ

brain

The Thinking Organ

Of all the organs in the human body, none is more vital than the brain. The brain is what gives us our identity. The acts of making decisions, solving problems, and identifying objects are all the direct responsibility of the brain.

The human brain stops growing when we are about six or seven years of age. When its growth is complete, the brain weighs about three kilograms. The brain is the most amazing and complex organ we know. It takes care of the creative things we do such as painting pictures, writing stories, designing buildings, and building computers. The brain processes information from all around us. When a traffic light turns red, we know not to cross the street, or when a dog growls at us, we know to keep away. Much of this information is stored in our memory. The brain also controls our emotions.

The largest part of the brain is called the cerebrum, which controls the muscles and processes sight, sound, taste, and smell messages. The left side of the cerebrum controls the right side of our body and the right side controls the left side of our body. The left side is dominant, which accounts for why most people are right-handed. Below the cerebrum is the cerebellum that controls balance and coordination. Near the cerebellum is the medulla oblongata that controls bodily functions such as breathing, swallowing, and vomiting. The hypothalamus controls our emotions, particularly anger and fear, and it controls body temperature, hunger, and thirst. The brain is also a main part of our nervous system.

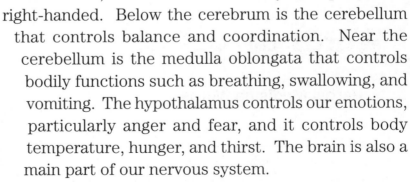

The brain has always been a mystery to humankind. We only know the basics of how it works. The more we study the brain and its function, the more we realize how complicated it is.

A. Circle the correct brain words for the descriptions.

1. the organ that determines who a person is:

   the brain   the cerebrum   the cerebellum

2. a feeling like happiness, anger, or fear:

   memory   identity   emotion

3. where something we remember from past experiences is stored:

   the hypothalamus   memory   the medulla oblongata

4. the brain is a part of this:

   the cerebrum

   the hypothalamus

   the nervous system

B. Unscramble the brain words and fill in the blanks.

The human brain is the most important 1._____ in the body.
                                                   grnoa

It is what gives us our 2._____ . The main 3._____
                               tdyienti   nnciftuo

of the brain is to process information. The brain also controls

our 4._____ , such as happiness and sadness. The
          nmoteiso

5._____ is the largest part of the brain. It is above the
   bcermuer

6._____ , which controls balance and coordination. The
   rmlleceube

7._____ controls emotions, body temperature, hunger, and
   pohalaumyths

thirst. The brain is also part of our 8._____ system.
                                                vnouers

C.　Read the clues and circle the brain words with the specified colours.

(red) : what the brain is

(blue) : what the brain gives us

(orange) : where information is stored

(green) : divided into left and right sides

(brown) : what controls body temperature

(purple) : what controls balance and coordination

(pink) : We study the brain and its _____ .

(yellow) : The brain belongs to the _____ system.

Brain Words

b	h	a	s								m	o	e	t
o	r	g	t	c	g	n	e	t	n	f	a	c	g	b
m	c	e	r	m	h	c	e	m	e	m	l	e	f	j
e	k	c	o	j	y	i	c	e	r	e	b	r	u	m
n	e	r	c	o	p	m	i	p	v	o	i	e	u	l
w	m	l	e	a	o	v	d	g	o	r	g	b	h	i
f	e	o	r	g	a	n	e	q	u	s	m	e	z	d
u	m	b	e	l	w	q	n	z	s	c	a	l	p	e
n	o	j	f	u	n	c	t	i	o	n	s	l	f	i
c	r	m	o	r	b	m	i	s	j	e	w	u	g	h
o	y	v	h	y	p	o	t	h	a	l	a	m	u	s
t	e	h	a	i	s	l	y	c	j	o	b	m	l	a

D. **Label the diagram with brain words and the words below.**

The Nervous System

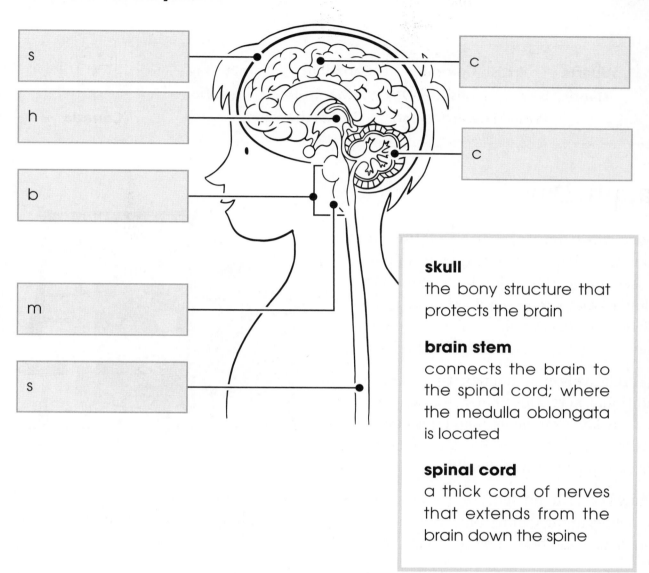

s

h

b

m

s

c

c

skull
the bony structure that protects the brain

brain stem
connects the brain to the spinal cord; where the medulla oblongata is located

spinal cord
a thick cord of nerves that extends from the brain down the spine

Words that I Have Learned

Brain Words

_____

_____

_____

_____

UNIT 5 **Canadian Words**

Alberta	British Columbia	Canadian	Family Day
Islander Day	Louis Riel Day	Manitoba	Ontario
Prince Edward Island	Saskatchewan

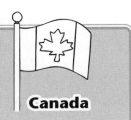

Canada

Family Day

Those who live in British Columbia, Alberta, Saskatchewan, and Ontario have the second or third Monday in February as Family Day each year. In Manitoba, it is called Louis Riel Day, and in Prince Edward Island, the holiday is called Islander Day.

As a relatively new holiday, there are no traditional activities that are associated with the day. Canadians spend this holiday in different ways, but as it is Family Day, it is best to spend it with family.

Family Day is in the midst of the bitter cold winter. If you enjoy outdoor activities, skating and tobogganing can be fun. But for most people, spending Family Day indoors makes more sense. So how about enjoying the holiday with your family this way?

Try baking cookies together. Make cookies of different shapes with cookie cutters, but leave the baking work for Mom and Dad, as the oven can be dangerously hot. You can help out afterwards by decorating and sampling the cookies to see if they are yummy enough.

Pick a movie to watch with your family. Tell them what the story is about and why it is fun to watch it. Then sit back and have a good time with Mom and Dad. Do not forget the freshly-baked cookies for snacks.

After dinner, how about playing a guessing game with your family? "With my little eye I spy" is simple and fun. Pick an object that everyone can see, but do not reveal what it is. Give a hint like "I spy with my little eye something that is blue", and let your family guess what you are spying on.

Have a fun-filled Family Day!

A. Fill in the blanks with the correct Canadian words.

Canadian Words

Prince Edward Island   Louis Riel Day   Canadians
Saskatchewan   Islander Day   Family Day

In the cold month of February, Canadians celebrate different holidays. In British Columbia, Alberta, 1._____ , and Ontario, 2._____ is celebrated on the second or third Monday of the month. In Manitoba, the holiday is called 3._____ . In 4._____ , the holiday is called 5._____ .

These holidays are not associated with traditional activities. 6._____ usually spend the holidays with their families. Some people enjoy outdoor activities while others prefer indoor activities.

B. Cross out the word that does not belong in each group. Then explain how the remaining words are related.

A
Saskatchewan
Toronto
Manitoba
Ontario

B
February
Islander Day
Louis Riel Day
Family Day

C
Alberta
Prince Edward Island
Canada
British Columbia

How the words are related:

A _____

B _____

C _____

C.   **Label the map of Canada with the correct province and territory names. Write their short forms on the map.**

Provinces

AB Alberta	**NS** Nova Scotia
BC British Columbia	**ON** Ontario
MB Manitoba	**PEI** Prince Edward Island
NB New Brunswick	**QC** Quebec
NL Newfoundland and Labrador	**SK** Saskatchewan

Territories

NT	Northwest Territories
NU	Nunavut
YT	Yukon

Canada

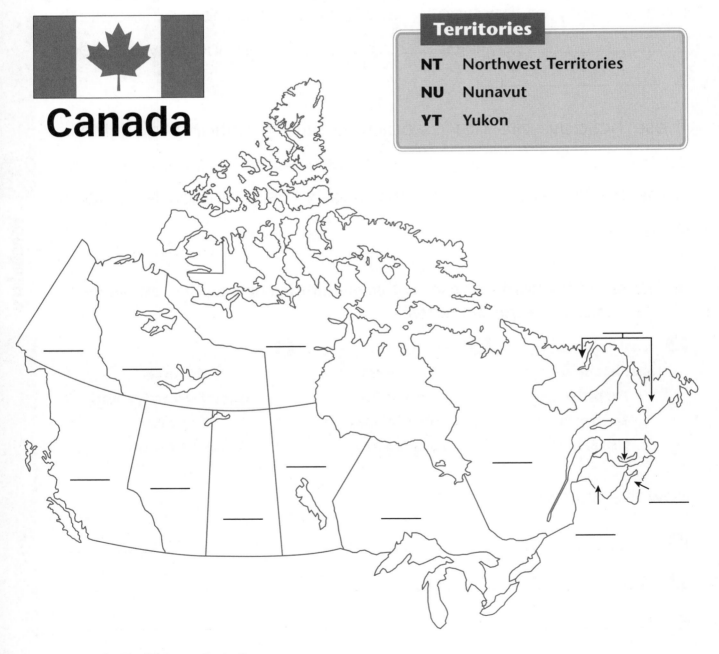

D. Match the provinces and territories of Canada with their capital cities.

⚜ **Canada**

Capital Cities

Provinces	
	Alberta
	British Columbia
	Manitoba
	New Brunswick
	Newfoundland and Labrador
	Nova Scotia
	Ontario
	Prince Edward Island
	Quebec
	Saskatchewan

Territories	
	Northwest Territories
	Nunavut
	Yukon

- Quebec City
- Regina
- Ottawa
- Edmonton
- Victoria
- Winnipeg
- Fredericton
- St. John's
- Halifax
- Toronto
- Charlottetown
- Whitehorse
- Iqaluit
- Yellowknife

Words that I Have Learned

Canadian Words

_____

_____

_____

_____

UNIT 6 Toy and Game Words

ball   blind man's bluff   hide-and-seek
hoop rolling   horseshoe pitching   rag doll
seesaw   swing   wooden soldier

toys and games

Toys and Games of Pioneer Canada

The toys children play with today are often highly technical and electronic. The children of pioneer Canada, however, did not have such advanced toys and games. Instead, they relied on making their own toys and creating fun, interactive games.

Although their toys were simple, pioneer children were never bored. After a hard day's work helping their parents on the homestead, they looked forward to free time to play. Many of their favourite games like blind man's bluff and hide-and-seek are still played today. A rope tied to a tree made a perfect swing and a plank over a saw-horse made an ideal seesaw. The swing and the seesaw are still very popular in playgrounds today.

Horseshoe pitching was also a popular game across Canada. It was not only a game for children. Adults took this game very seriously and competitions between neighbours and towns were common.

Since there were no manufactured toys available to pioneer children, they had to be very creative when it came to making their own toys. A simple ball was made out of a stuffed pig's bladder, which was sturdy enough to be kicked around the field without breaking open. Hoop rolling was also a popular game. An iron or a wooden hoop and a stick were all that was needed.

Many games were useful in helping boys and girls prepare for adult life. Girls made rag dolls and sewed clothing. Boys went hunting and fishing with their fathers. Making a strong fishing rod out of a tree branch was an important skill. Boys were skilled with knives and learned the art of carving, which was useful for making toys, like wooden soldiers, for their younger brothers and sisters.

Even though pioneer children lived without television and computers, life was never dull. There was always work to do, fields and streams to play in, and the creative art of toy making to keep them busy.

A. Identify and write the names of the toys and games.

1.

_____

2.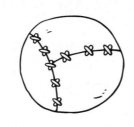

_____

3.

_____

4.

_____

5.

6.

_____

7.

_____

8.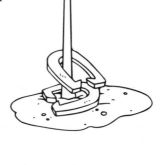

_____

9.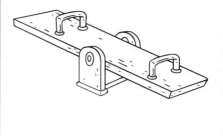

_____

Section **3**

Vocabulary

B. Circle the adjectives that are used to describe toys and games in the passage. Then write the correct adjectives for the definitions.

Adjectives Used to Describe Toys and Games

creative   advanced   bored   free   interactive

dull   simple   manufactured   busy   electronic

skilled   hard   fun   technical   important

1. involving more than one person in doing something together or acting upon each other _____

2. not complicated _____

3. involving the use of a computer _____

4. ahead in development; well-developed _____

5. involving new and original ideas _____

6. produced on a large scale _____

7. enjoyable; entertaining _____

8. relating to science or industry _____

C. Look up the meanings of the adjectives. Then use each of them in a sentence to describe a toy or a game.

durable _____

_____

innovative _____

_____

D. Match the descriptions of the toys and games with the correct pictures.

Ⓐ a game with two teams pulling at opposite ends of a rope, each team trying to drag the other team over a line between them

Ⓑ a large hoop played by moving one's waist and hips to make it rotate around the body

Ⓒ a game in which a player throws an object into a group of squares drawn on the ground and then hops through the squares to pick up the object

Ⓓ a game played by putting many small, irregularly shaped pieces together to form a picture

Toys and Games

jigsaw puzzle ◯

tug of war ◯

hula hoop ◯

hopscotch ◯

Words that I Have Learned

Toy and Game Words

_____

_____

_____

_____

UNIT

7

Ancient Civilization Words

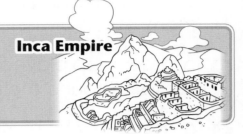

architecture   army   canal   conqueror
drainage   fortress   highland   punishment
resource   territory   warrior

Inca Empire

The Inca Empire

Between 1200 and 1535 CE, the Inca built the largest empire in South America, extending from the equator to the Pacific coast of Chile. The Inca were fierce warriors with a strong and powerful army. However, their prosperity came to a tragic end when the Spanish conquerors took over their territory.

The architecture of the Inca cities still amazes and puzzles most scientists. The Inca built their cities and fortresses on highlands and on the steep slopes of the Andes Mountains. Stone steps lead up to the top of the cities. The stone blocks weighing several tons are fit together so tightly that not even a razor blade can fit through them. Their homes were made from the same stone material and had grass rooftops.

The Inca developed sophisticated drainage systems and canals to expand their crop resources. They also reared llamas for meat and transportation. There were more than enough resources for everyone. The Inca had a good road system to connect the villages too. The roads were lined with barriers to prevent people from falling down the cliffs.

The Inca were not only fierce warriors but they also had a violent punishment system. People who committed theft would be severely punished. Those who committed murder would be sentenced to death.

Ironically, though, the 40 000-member army of the Inca was destroyed by a 180-member Spanish army led by Francisco Pizarro. The Inca warriors were simply no match for the Spanish guns. By 1535, the Inca society was completely wiped out. Now, only a few traces of Inca ways remain in the native culture as it exists today.

A. Complete the crossword puzzle with ancient civilization words.

Across

- **A** a soldier, a fighter
- **B** an area of land belonging to a group
- **C** the style and organization of buildings
- **D** a person who takes over a place and its people

Down

- **1** a strong building or an organized group of strong buildings defending an area from attack
- **2** a penalty for an offence
- **3** a supply of essential items
- **4** an artificial waterway
- **5** an organized group of warriors

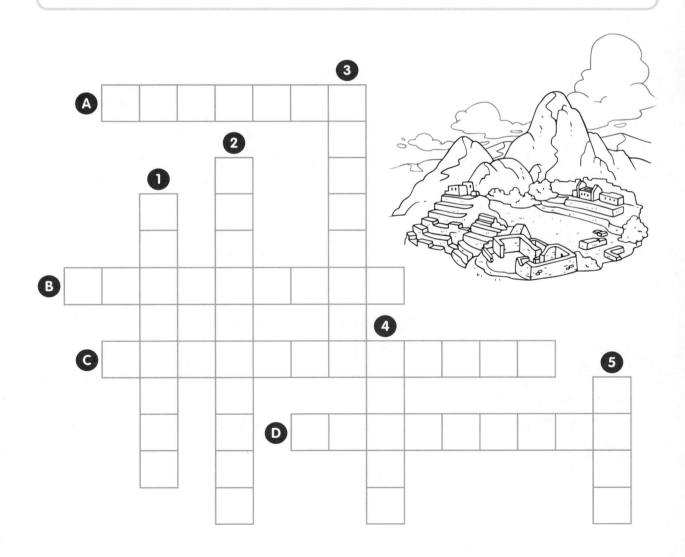

B.   Identify and label the ancient civilizations.

More Ancient Civilizations

Ancient China   Ancient Egypt   Ancient Greece

Ancient Rome   Ancient Mesopotamia

1. _____

- located in today's Rome
- began the Roman Republic
- Julius Caesar ended the Roman Republic

2. _____

- began around the Yellow River
- located in today's China
- many inventions including paper and the compass

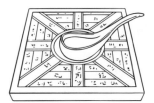

3. _____

- located along the Nile River
- ruled by pharaohs
- built pyramids as tombs for pharaohs

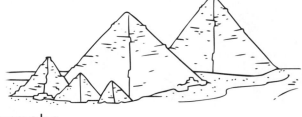

4. _____

- famous people including Plato, Pythagoras, and Alexander the Great
- created the ancient Olympics
- built the Parthenon in the city of Athens

5. _____

- covered today's Iran, Syria, and Turkey
- referred to as the Cradle of Civilization
- Babylon being its most famous city

C. Circle the correct ancient civilization words to complete the sentences.

1. The cities and fortresses of the Inca Empire were built on **plateaus / highlands** .

2. To expand their crop resources, the Inca had sophisticated **road / drainage** systems.

3. Ancient **Greece / Mesopotamia** was the first civilization in the world.

4. Every year, many tourists visit the **Parthenon / Great Pyramid** , which was originally a temple in Athens built in Ancient Greece.

5. Many ancient civilizations developed along rivers. One example is Ancient Egypt, which was along the **Yellow / Nile** River.

6. Paper, printing, silk, and the compass are among the many inventions of Ancient **China / Egypt** .

7. The Olympic Games originated in Ancient **Greece / China** thousands of years ago.

Words that I Have Learned

Ancient Civilization Words

_____

_____

_____

_____

UNIT

8 Money Words

barter   bead   cash   credit card
currency   debit card   jewellery   metal
payment   personal cheque   shell

money

The Origins of Money

When we want to make a purchase today, we use money. We have many options as to how we pay with money. We can use a credit card, a debit card, a personal cheque, or cash.

In ancient times, when money was non-existent, people bartered (traded) goods and services for other goods and services that they needed. Items such as shells, beads, metal, gold, jewellery, feathers, and tools were always welcome in a trade. Instead of simply trading goods and services, a crude form of currency was established by tribes around the world.

In Africa and Asia, shells were used as currency while in North America, the Indigenous Peoples used necklaces and headdresses in place of money. In Central Africa, copper rods called congas were used as currency. For ten of these rods, a native could buy himself a wife. In China, bronze miniatures were used to purchase the actual articles they represented. For example, a tiny replica of a tool would be used to purchase that exact tool. Probably the most popular form of currency was the use of animals. Cattle, pigs, and camels are still used today to purchase products or make payments by some tribes in Asia.

However, with the growth of cities, standard forms of payment became necessary to regulate the value of goods. The barter method worked nicely between individuals or in a village setting, but it lacked consistency. There was no standard by which a person could measure the value of what they were buying. It was difficult to be sure that the deal was fair. Often the one who was the shrewdest dealer profited most. It became necessary to establish a regular system. This marked the beginning of money as we know it today.

A. Unscramble the money words with the help of the definition clues.

1. letma _____ : a strong and solid substance

2. cunyrerc _____ : a system of money used in a country

3. quehec _____ : a printed form to make a payment from one's bank account

4. rabrte _____ : exchange goods

5. bedit _____ : money taken from a bank account

6. weejellyr _____ : rings, necklaces, etc. made from precious stones or metals

B. Fill in the blanks with the correct money words.

We use 1._____ to purchase items when we go shopping. In ancient times, money did not exist. People would trade goods and services for other goods and services. Popular items used in trading include shells, 2._____ , metal, gold, jewellery, 3._____ , and tools. This 4._____ method worked well between individuals or in a village. However, it was not always fair. A regular system of 5._____ was established over time. Today, when we need to pay for things we buy, we can use different ways such as 6._____ , a personal 7._____ , a 8._____ card, or a 9._____ card. The way we measure currency today has become highly regulated and efficient.

C. Write the names and values of the Canadian currency.

1.

penny *

1¢

_____

_____

5 CENTS CANADA 1987

_____

CANADA DOLLAR

_____

dime

_____

CANADA 2 DOLLARS

_____

2. _____ five-dollar bill _____ ; ___$5___

3. _____ ; _____

4. _____ ; _____

5. _____ ; _____

6. _____ ; _____

* The Canadian penny is no longer distributed. However, existing pennies can still be used as currency. Like different forms of currency from ancient times, regulated money is still evolving.

D. Circle the money words in the word search.

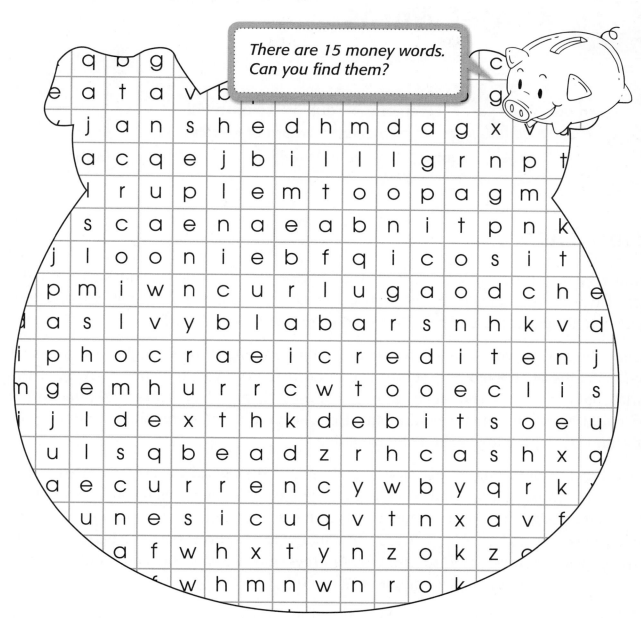

There are 15 money words. Can you find them?

q	p	g									c
e	a	t	a	v	b					g	
j	a	n	s	h	e	d	h	m	d	a	g	x
a	c	q	e	j	b	i	l	l	l	g	r	n	p	t
l	r	u	p	l	e	m	t	o	o	p	a	g	m
s	c	a	e	n	a	e	a	b	n	i	t	p	n	k
j	l	o	o	n	i	e	b	f	q	i	c	o	s	i	t
p	m	i	w	n	c	u	r	l	u	g	a	o	d	c	h	e
a	s	l	v	y	b	l	a	b	a	r	s	n	h	k	v	d
i	p	h	o	c	r	a	e	i	c	r	e	d	i	t	e	n	j
n	g	e	m	h	u	r	r	c	w	t	o	o	e	c	l	i	s
i	j	l	d	e	x	t	h	k	d	e	b	i	t	s	o	e	u
u	l	s	q	b	e	a	d	z	r	h	c	a	s	h	x	q
a	e	c	u	r	r	e	n	c	y	w	b	y	q	r	k
u	n	e	s	i	c	u	q	v	t	n	x	a	v	f
a	f	w	h	x	t	y	n	z	o	k	z	c
w	h	m	n	w	n	r	o	k

Section 3 Vocabulary

Words that I Have Learned

Money Words

_____

_____

_____

_____

UNIT 9

Knight Words

armour	castle	ceremony	dub	knighthood
lance	Middle Ages	nobleman	oath of chivalry
page	squire	sword	weapon

knight

I Dub Thee. . .

Edward was a fortunate boy because he was born the son of a nobleman during the Middle Ages. He knew that one day he would become a knight, just like his father. He dreamed of the knighting ceremony where he would be dubbed "Sir Edward".

Finally, the day arrived when Edward could start training to be a knight. He was sent from his home at the age of seven to live in Lord Henry's castle. Upon arriving at the castle, the first level of training as a "page" began. Edward learned how to hunt with a falcon and handle weapons and armour. He also spent much of his time mounted on a horse and strengthening his body by wrestling.

Edward managed to endure life as a "page" and, at the age of 14, he graduated to the next level of training as a "squire". Fighting practice was one of his favourite exercises. He was also assigned to be a personal servant for Sir Andrew. Along with caring for his knight's weapons and armour, Edward accompanied Sir Andrew onto the battlefield. On many occasions, Edward had to assist Sir Andrew when he was knocked off his horse or wounded by an opponent's lance.

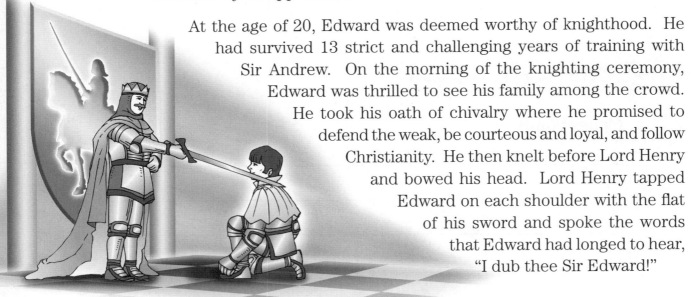

At the age of 20, Edward was deemed worthy of knighthood. He had survived 13 strict and challenging years of training with Sir Andrew. On the morning of the knighting ceremony, Edward was thrilled to see his family among the crowd. He took his oath of chivalry where he promised to defend the weak, be courteous and loyal, and follow Christianity. He then knelt before Lord Henry and bowed his head. Lord Henry tapped Edward on each shoulder with the flat of his sword and spoke the words that Edward had longed to hear, "I dub thee Sir Edward!"

A. Circle the correct knight words for the descriptions.

1. a formal occasion:

    oath   page   ceremony

2. a religion:

    Middle Ages   Christianity   knighthood

3. an honourable man of high ranking:

    page   squire   nobleman

4. a metal covering to protect the body:

    armour   weapon   castle

5. to give someone a name or a title:

    dub   oath   knighthood

6. a formal and sincere promise:

    ceremony   squire   oath

7. a mounted soldier in armour serving a lord:

    page   squire   knight

8. the first level of knight training:

    knighthood   page   chivalry

9. a weapon with a long, thin pole and a pointed head:

sword

armour

lance

B. **Cross out the word that does not belong on each shield. Then explain how the remaining words are related.**

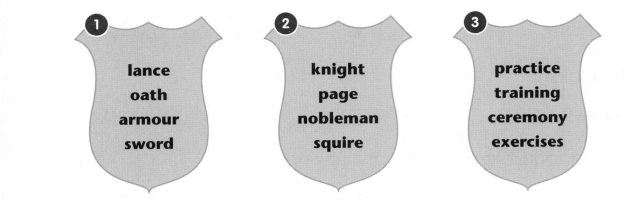

1 _____

2 _____

3 _____

C. **Read the descriptions and write the knight words in the correct boxes.**

Knight Words

page   squire   knight

1.	• assigned to be a personal servant of a knight • took care of the knight's weapons and armour • accompanied the knight onto the battlefield
2.	• took an oath of chivalry during the knighting ceremony • promised to defend the weak
3.	• learned how to hunt with a falcon • learned how to handle weapons • strengthened his body by wrestling

D. Fill in the blanks with the correct knight words.

More Knight Words

| purification | knighting | fasting |
| altar | rituals | lord | chapel |

After years of training, a squire should have mastered his fighting skills and be deemed worthy of knighthood. There were many 1._____ to perform before and during the knighting ceremony. The night before the ceremony, the squire would dress himself in white. He would spend the night in the 2._____ of the castle, 3._____ and praying, while keeping watch over his armour and weapons that were displayed on the 4._____ . In the morning, the squire would bathe as a symbol of 5._____ . He would then dress in the traditional 6._____ colours of red, white, and brown. The fast was over and he would be permitted to eat breakfast. During the ceremony, he would take his oath of chivalry after which he would be dubbed by the 7._____ .

Words that I Have Learned

Knight Words

_____

_____

_____

breeze	fall	fog	frost	hail
ice	lightning	rain	snow	
summer	sun	thunder	wind	

weather

A Fairy's Mistake

One day, two fairies named Autumn and Flora were painting fall colours in the forest. Flora brushed on too much orange accidentally. She had meant to mix it up with yellow, so she pulled out her magic cloth to rub it out. Then a light breeze tickled her and she dropped her cloth. Suddenly the breeze turned into a strong wind and it whirled off with the magic cloth.

The other fairies were upset with Flora. Because she was behind in her leaf-colouring, the leaf-dropping fairy would be late, which meant that the frost fairy would be late too, and so on. Not only were the other fairies angry with her, the trees were confused about their true colours; they thought it was still summer! Speaking of colours, even the sun started to shine with an angry, red hue. Because the trees were not the right colour, the sun did not know how high in the sky it should be. As a result of all the confusion, the weather was unpredictable. One morning there was snow on the ground, but that same night there was rain, thunder, and lightning! The next day, it was even stranger; there was so much fog that Flora could barely see, and then the sky started to hail tiny droplets of ice! Flora had no idea how important her job truly was.

Flora was determined to find her cloth and finish her job. She searched for her cloth for a whole week before she found it.

Things were then back to normal. Flora was busy painting her browns and reds on the leaves. When she made a mistake, she rubbed it out with her cloth. Flora learned a very big lesson from losing her cloth. It was not the cloth that was magic; it was Flora all along!

A. Write the correct weather word for each picture.

1.

_____

2.

_____

3.

_____

4.

_____

5.

_____

6.

_____

7.

_____

8.

_____

9.

_____

B. Match the weather words with their descriptions. Write the letters.

1. rain _____

2. fog _____

3. wind _____

4. thunder _____

5. frost _____

6. snow _____

7. hail _____

8. breeze _____

A. small balls of ice that fall from clouds

B. ice crystals that form on a surface

C. a light, gentle wind

D. water drops that fall from clouds

E. soft, light flakes of ice falling from the sky

F. moving air

G. a cloud close to the ground that reduces visibility

H. the explosive sound of air expanding as it is heated by lightning

C.   Name the seasons and circle the correct weather words.

1.

- around March – June
- **hot / warm** days and cool nights
- plants begin to **grow / wither**
- trees start to **die / bud**

2.

- around July – August
- **hot / cold** and **humid / dry**
- long hours of **darkness / daylight**
- lots of **rain / snow**

3.

- around September – November
- **hot / cool** days and nights
- **breezy / rainy**
- leaves change colour and fall

4.

- around December – February
- **hot / cold** and **humid / dry**
- long hours of **darkness / daylight**
- lots of **rain / snow**

D. Put the weather words in the correct categories. Then add two more words to each category.

More Weather Words

blast

draft

drizzle

drought

freezing rain

gale

gust

heat wave

hurricane

ice pellet

ice storm

sleet

Precipitation

_____

_____

Wind

_____

_____

Extreme Weather Condition

_____

_____

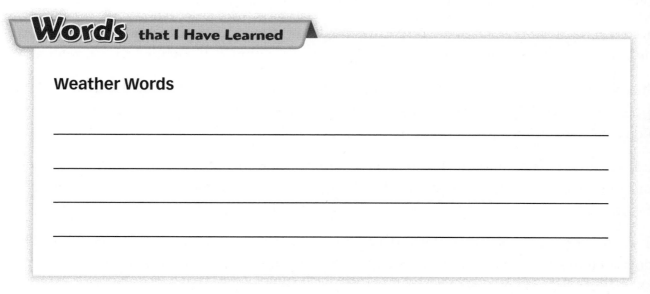

Words that I Have Learned

Weather Words

_____

_____

_____

_____

UNIT 11 Sport Words

athlete	badminton	basketball	birdie
court	cross-country meet	high jump	
shot put	soccer	track and field	volleyball

sports

A Sporty Gal

Laura is an incredible athlete who would be involved in every extra-curricular activity year round if she could have her way. However, her parents view it differently. As it is, Laura's parents do an amazing juggling act of schedules to drop off and pick up Laura at practice and game locations.

In the fall, Laura runs every day during her lunch hour or after school, training for cross-country meets where she races a distance of over one kilometre. Following the cross-country season comes volleyball, where Laura is the "setter", considered the most important position on the court.

Right after the winter holidays, Laura gets in shape for the basketball season. She plays the position of guard, which means she is awesome at dribbling the ball.

As soon as spring arrives comes the badminton team. Laura plays singles or doubles, where she tries to strategically shoot the "birdie" on the opponent's side where it is unreachable.

Finally, near the end of the school year is the track and field season. Laura has great upper body strength and excels at shot put. She also succeeds in high jump, where she does the "Fosbury Flop" technique.

Laura's all-star soccer team kicks in just before summer begins. She plays a defence position, responsible for protecting her team's end of the field so that the other team does not score.

As a result of Laura's jammed packed athletic life, she does not have much free time. This sporty gal does not seem to mind though because she is crazy about sports.

A. Look at the pictures and name the sports.

1.

2.

3.

_____

4.

_____

5.

_____

_____

_____

B. Fill in the blanks with the correct sport words.

Laura loves sports and she is an incredible 1._____ . She works hard all year round to train for her favourite 2._____ . During the fall, Laura runs every day to prepare for 3._____ meets where she races for long distances. Another sport that Laura plays in the fall is 4._____ . Laura is the setter, which is a very important position on the team. Training for the 5._____ season comes right after the winter holidays. Laura is great at dribbling the ball so she plays the position of guard. In spring, Laura joins the 6._____ team, where she trains to strategically shoot the birdie to an unreachable position on the opponent's side. 7._____ season comes near the end of the school year. Laura's upper body strength makes her excel in 8._____ . Her "Fosbury Flop" technique also leads to her success in 9._____ . In the summer, Laura plays a defence position with her all-star 10._____ team. Laura is really an awesome sporty gal!

C. **Complete the crossword puzzle with sport words from the story.**

Across

A learning and practising the skills of a sport

B a position on a soccer team

C a group of athletes

D where volleyball is played

E a position on a basketball team

Down

1 the "Fosbury Flop" _____

2 bouncing a basketball

3 a position on a volleyball team

4 badminton equipment

5 a track and field event

D. Match the sports with their equipment.

More Sports

 golf •

 tennis •

 hockey •

 archery •

 bowling •

 baseball •

Sport Equipment

• skates

• racket

• puck

• arrow

• bat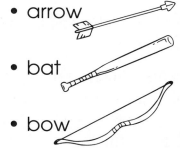

• bow

• net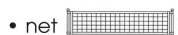

• pins

• club

Words that I Have Learned

Sport Words

_____

_____

_____

_____

UNIT

12 Gardening Words

compost determinate fruit indeterminate manure mulch nursery organic soil sunlight transplant weed	 **tomatoes**

How to Grow Tomatoes

Growing tomatoes is not too difficult, but it requires patience as they take quite a long time to grow.

For a first-timer, it is better to get small tomato plants from a nursery and transplant them. Tomato plants grow best in soil that is rich in organic matter. If you do not make your own compost, you should buy some composted manure from stores and mix it into the soil. Place the tomato plants where there is sunlight for seven hours or more every day.

Place a mulch of straw or pine needles to control weeds and keep the soil moist during dry weather. For the first ten days, water each plant with about half a litre of warm water every day. Increase the amount of water as the plants grow larger. In hot and dry weather, you should water them even more frequently.

Consider buying cages to help the plants grow. A cage should be at least 1.2 metres tall, or even taller if your tomato plants grow well. There are two types of tomato plants: determinate and indeterminate. A determinate tomato plant grows to a certain size and then slows or stops its growth. An indeterminate plant just keeps growing and spreading out.

Fruit should appear about 60 days after transplanting. Tomato plants usually have small, green fruit to start. When the fruit reaches a good size with bright colour, it is ripe and ready to pick. Be careful of not letting it become too ripe or it will become very soft. Watch out for birds and raccoons, as they love ripe tomatoes as much as we do!

A. **Fill in the blanks with the correct gardening words. Then put the instructions in the correct order by numbering the steps from 1 to 6.**

Steps to Planting Tomatoes

Water the _____ with warm water every day.

Pick the _____ once it is a bright colour and ripe.

Buy plants from a _____ and transplant them.

Place a _____ of straw or pine needles to keep the _____ moist.

Mix _____ or composted _____ into the soil.

Place the tomato plants where there is _____ for at least seven hours a day.

B. **Match the gardening words with their definitions. Write the letters.**

1. compost   _____

2. organic   _____

3. manure   _____

4. mulch   _____

5. nursery   _____

6. determinate   _____

7. indeterminate   _____

A. a plant that grows to a certain size

B. a material spread over soil to insulate it

C. derived from living and natural matter

D. a plant that keeps growing and spreading out

E. animal dung used for fertilizing soil

F. decayed organic matter used as plant fertilizer

G. a place where young plants are grown for sale

C. **Read the descriptions and write the parts of the plants. Then label the diagram of the tomato plant.**

Parts of a Plant

flower   fruit   leaf   root   seed   stem

1. _____ : anchors the plant to the ground; takes water and nutrients from the soil

2. _____ : the sweet and soft product of a plant that contains seeds and can be eaten as food

3. _____ : attached to the stem of a plant; turns sunlight into food for the plant

4. _____ : the seed-producing part of a plant; attracts birds and insects to spread its pollen

5. _____ : the main body of a plant; transports water and nutrients throughout the plant

6. _____ : grows into a new plant

7. **The Tomato Plant**

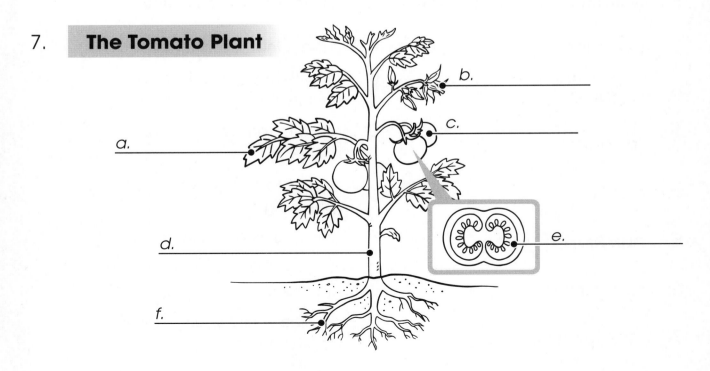

D. Unscramble the gardening words and write them on the lines.

Gardening Tools

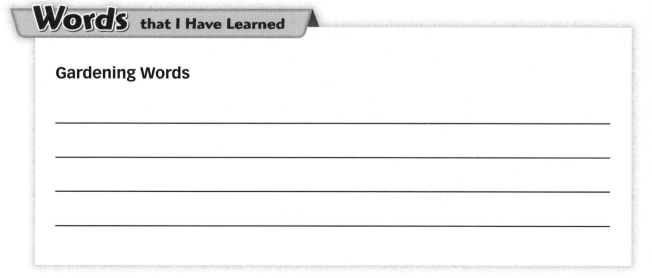

1. _____ krae

2. _____ loevgs

3. _____ sheo

4. _____ wlna   _____ mwero

5. _____ igntware   _____ nac

6. _____ trweol   _____ nerspur

Words that I Have Learned

Gardening Words

_____

_____

_____

_____

UNIT 13 Musical Instrument Words

clarinet   drums   flute   guitar
piano   saxophone   trombone
trumpet   violin

musical instruments

Summer Music Camps

Emir and Marcus both love music and participate in their school's band. During the summer holidays, they went to different music camps. They were excited to go to music camps during the summer to learn new skills and play new instruments.

Emir's camp was fun, but it was also a lot of work. His music camp was three weeks long. Each week he got to try a new instrument while still practising his own instrument. He tried the trombone, the drums, and the clarinet. That was the hard part. Playing a new instrument each week was very challenging. He did have fun playing his own instrument, the violin, and he improved a lot too!

Marcus went to Mackie Lake Music Camp. At his camp, they played a little bit of music for fun during the day, and they did a lot of swimming and kayaking too. When it got dark, the campers would sit around the campfire and play the guitar while singing songs. Marcus thought that the guitar instructor was very good. He was happy that the instructor helped him improve his guitar skills. For the mid-camp concert, Marcus learned how to play the piano, the saxophone, the flute, and the trumpet! It was hard work but he had a lot of fun learning how to play these new instruments.

Emir and Marcus were excited to see each other again after they got home from their summer music camps. They had both learned so much and improved at playing their own instruments. When they got together again, they played their instruments and practised their music skills even more!

A. Identify and write the names of the musical instruments.

1.

_____

2.

_____

3.

_____

4.

_____

5.

_____

6.

_____

7.

_____

8.

_____

B. **Read the descriptions and write the types of musical instruments. Then sort the instruments by writing the letters in the circles.**

Types of Musical Instruments

Brass   Percussion

Woodwind   String

_____ Instrument
• played by blowing into the reed of the instrument and pressing different keys to change the pitch of the notes

e.g. ◯ , ◯ , and ◯

_____ Instrument
• played by placing the lips against or inside the cup of a metal mouthpiece and blowing into the instrument by buzzing the lips

e.g. ◯ and ◯

_____ Instrument
• played by plucking or strumming the strings of the instrument, or played with a bow

e.g. ◯ and ◯

_____ Instrument
• played by hitting the instrument by hand or with sticks, or by shaking the instrument

e.g. ◯ and ◯

A guitar   **B** violin

C flute   **D** trombone

E drums   **F** clarinet

G piano   **H** trumpet

I saxophone

C. Unscramble the musical instrument words. Then put them in the correct categories by writing the numbers on the lines.

1.

_____
aphr

2.

_____
ramasca

3.

_____
drereroc

4.

_____
reFchn onhr

5.

_____
ritglean

6.
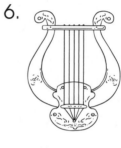

_____
yrle

Types of Musical Instruments

Brass: _____   Percussion: _____

String: _____   Woodwind: _____

Words that I Have Learned

Musical Instrument Words

_____

_____

_____

_____

UNIT 14 Technology Words

camera   cellphone   computer   e-reader
Internet   laptop   modem
router   tablet   telephone   Wi-Fi

technological devices

Claire's Class Trip

Claire was excited to go on a field trip with her class to a museum. Claire is fascinated by science and technology and enjoys learning about this subject in school.

The first type of technology Claire's class learned about was the computer. Claire learned that the computer used to be an incredibly large machine that could take up an entire room! She was surprised to learn that early versions of the computer did not have the Internet. When the Internet was created, computers could only connect to it through phone lines using two devices called a router and a modem. Today, most computers access the Internet through a wireless connection known as Wi-Fi. Computers today are also much smaller and more portable than early computers. They come in different shapes and sizes, such as desktop and laptop computers.

Claire was also interested in learning about the history of the telephone. Before her visit to the museum, when Claire thought of a telephone, she thought of a cellphone. She likes to use her dad's cellphone to play games and to take pictures with the cellphone's camera. However, unlike the modern cellphone, the early telephone could only be used for calling people. It was connected to a landline which means that it had to be attached to an outlet on the wall. Claire thinks it is amazing that technology has advanced so much that all of these technological tools can now be combined into one device. For example, a tablet functions as a computer, a cellphone, a camera, and an e-reader all at once!

After learning all of these interesting things about technology, Claire thinks that she might want to be a computer scientist when she grows up!

An Early Invention – COMPUTER

A. Match the technology words with the definitions.

1. telephone •
2. Internet •
3. camera •
4. laptop •
5. cellphone •
6. computer •
7. Wi-Fi •
8. tablet •

• a device for taking photographs

• a worldwide system of computer networks

• a device that transmits sound

• a wireless Internet connection

• a portable computer that fits on your lap

• a small portable computer with a touch screen

• a hand-held mobile telephone

• an information processing system

B. Write the technology words in the correct parts of the diagram.

television

Walkman

computer

tablet

cassette

telephone

Wi-Fi

e-reader

radio

typewriter

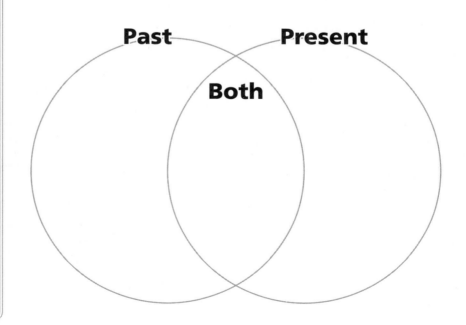

Past   Present

Both

C. **Name the technological devices. Then identify them as past or present technology. Write "past" or "present" in the boxes.**

Technological Devices

1. _____

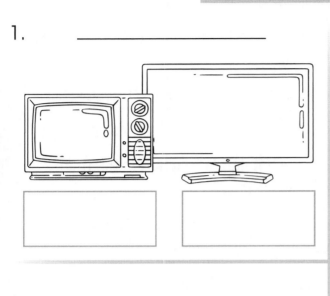

2. _____

3. _____

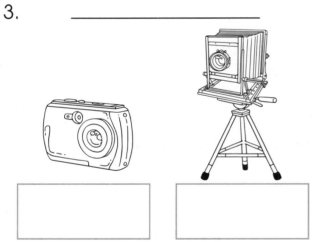

4. _____

5. _____

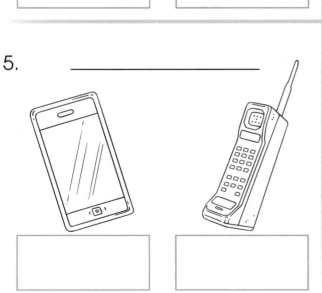

D. Fill in the blanks with the correct technology words.

On Claire's birthday, her parents bought her a 1._____ . Claire was so excited to use her new computer. Once she turned it on, she tried to connect to the 2._____ using the 3._____ connection in her home. Her computer failed to connect several times and Claire realized that the 4._____ and the 5._____ that connect to the Internet were not plugged into the wall! After Claire solved the problem, she was able to connect to the Internet and use different apps. She took pictures with the computer's 6._____ and read books online using her computer's 7._____ app.

Words that I Have Learned

Technology Words

_____

_____

_____

_____

A. Circle the answers.

1. My mother's gold _____ was stolen.

   debit card

   jewellery

   personal cheque

2. Camouflage is _____ .

   a predator

   an organism

   an adaptation

3. Which playground equipment is this?

   a seesaw

   a rag doll

   a swing

   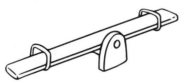

4. Butterflies blending into their background is a form of _____ .

   catching prey

   habitat

   camouflage

5. A good _____ system can prevent flooding.

   farming

   army

   drainage

6. What game is this?

   tug of war

   hopscotch

   jigsaw puzzle

7. What is a heavily protected building called?

   a home

   a fortress

   a tunnel

8. What type of oath does a knight take?

   oath of chivalry

   oath of armour

   oath of lance

9. An animal's natural environment is its _____ .

   forest

   house

   habitat

10. What toy is this?

    a wooden soldier

    a rag doll

    a mechanical toy

11. Which is used as plant fertilizer?

    compost

    weeds

    sunlight

12. What is one level higher than a page?

    a knight

    a nobleman

    a squire

13. What is an artificial waterway called?

    a canal

    a river

    a pond

14. Every country has its own _____ .

    cash

    currency

    credit card

15. An animal that hunts another is _____ .

    a herbivore

    the prey

    a predator

16. What type of protective gear is this?

    a robe

    an armour

    a cape

Brain and Medical Words

B.   Put the words in order to form sentences. Then write the underlined words in the correct boxes.

1.   <u>wound</u> the was not properly <u>disinfected</u>

   _____

2.   <u>congenital</u> can diseases defence lower

   _____

3.   <u>brain</u> the a organ vital is

   _____

4.   on her the <u>surgeon</u> <u>spinal cord</u> operated

   _____

5.   <u>infection</u> had the spread his to <u>lungs</u>

   _____

6.   the birds <u>cerebellum</u> of highly is developed

   _____

7.   loss <u>memory</u> of Susie's destroyed her identity

   _____

8.   vitamins the to the doctor <u>nervous system</u> prescribed strengthen

   _____

Brain Word 

Medical Word

Technology, Musical Instrument, and Sport Words

C. Read the story. Then fill in the blanks with the correct words.

Technology Word	Musical Instrument Word	Sport Word
computer Wi-Fi tablet camera router	guitar drums violin trumpet clarinet	tennis athlete soccer volleyball cross-country

Josh, Jack, and Janet were three siblings with very different interests.

Josh loved to spend time looking up information on his c_____ , taking pictures with his c_____ , and learning about the way a r_____ works to provide W_____ . His father always relied on him to fix his t_____ .

Jack, on the other hand, had a passion for music. He could play the c_____ and the d_____ , but his favourites were the g_____ and the v_____ . His mother was very proud of him but she did not let him play the loud t_____ in the house!

Janet loved sports and wanted to be the best a_____ in school. She played s_____ on the weekends, t_____ on Mondays, v_____ on Tuesdays, and ran around the court on Thursdays to practise for the c_____ meet. Because of her love of sports, her parents and brothers all joked about how she always kept them on their toes.

Canadian and Weather Words

D. Write the names of the provinces and the territories of Canada next to their short forms.

Map of Canada

Provinces

AB _____

BC _____

MB _____

NB _____

NL _____

NS _____

ON _____

PEI _____

QC _____

SK _____

Territories

NT _____

NU _____

YT _____

E. Match the pictures with the weather words.

Weather Words

| hail | rain | fog |
| wind | lightning | |

1.

2.

3.

4.

Gardening and Herbal Medicine Words

F. Use the diagram to solve the crossword puzzle.

Life Cycle of the Apple Tree

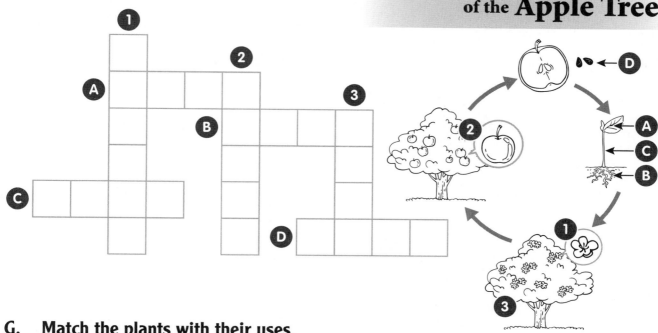

G. Match the plants with their uses.

Herbal Medicine

foxglove leaves

turmeric

rosemary

aloe vera

cinchona tree bark

sunflower

Use

- treats malaria
- treats colds and coughs
- prevents memory loss
- treat heart conditions
- controls stiffness, irritation, and pain
- reduces dryness and sunburn damage

Section 4

Reading and Writing

UNIT 1

Not a Typical Grandma

May 17, 2019

Dear Grams,

I miss you. I was thinking today about how you're not a typical grandma. For example, I don't call you Grandma because you think it makes you sound "over the hill". That's why I call you Grammy or Grams.

You don't look like a typical grandma either because you have long, beautiful, brown hair. When you go swimming or hiking, you put your hair up in a ponytail and you look like a Barbie doll. You also have great fashion sense. Your wardrobe is exploding with cool outfits. When it comes to attire for an elaborate occasion, you are always "dressed to the nines".

You never live in one place for a long time like a typical grandma. Mom says you have "ants in your pants" and that's why you are always travelling the world. Last year, you lived in Australia when you were studying at a university, and before that, you were going on safari adventures in South Africa. Now that you live in Toronto and are writing a book, I'm going to come visit you!

There are so many things that we can do together. I know you love rollerblading, whitewater rafting, mountain climbing, and tobogganing. We could do one of those things, or we can try horseback riding. I know how much you like to "go like the wind".

You aren't a typical grandma, but you're a lot of other wonderful things. Grams, you're the "greatest thing since sliced bread".

Love,
Emily

A. Circle the answers.

1. To whom is the letter addressed?

   Emily

   Grams

   Grandpa

2. How does Emily repeatedly describe her grandma?

   adventurous

   like a Barbie doll

   not typical

3. When does Emily's grandma put her hair up in a ponytail?

   when she swims

   when she writes

   when she rollerblades

4. Where was Emily's grandma last year?

   in Australia

   in South Africa

   in Toronto

B. Answer the questions.

1. What is the purpose of this letter?

   _____

2. What sports does Emily's grandma love that make her not a typical grandma?

   _____

3. What do these phrases mean?

   over the hill: _____

   dressed to the nines: _____

    Look for context clues to get the meanings.

   ants in your pants: _____

   go like the wind: _____

   greatest thing since sliced bread: _____

C. **Imagine that you are going to write a letter to your grandparent. Brainstorm ideas for your letter below.**

 This is a friendly letter. The purpose of a friendly letter is to communicate, for example, to give or ask information, to make a request, or to say thank you.

My Ideas for a Friendly Letter

 I am writing to _____

 I want to tell him/her...

 I want to ask him/her...

 I want to thank him/her...

D. Write a friendly letter to your grandparent using your ideas from (C).

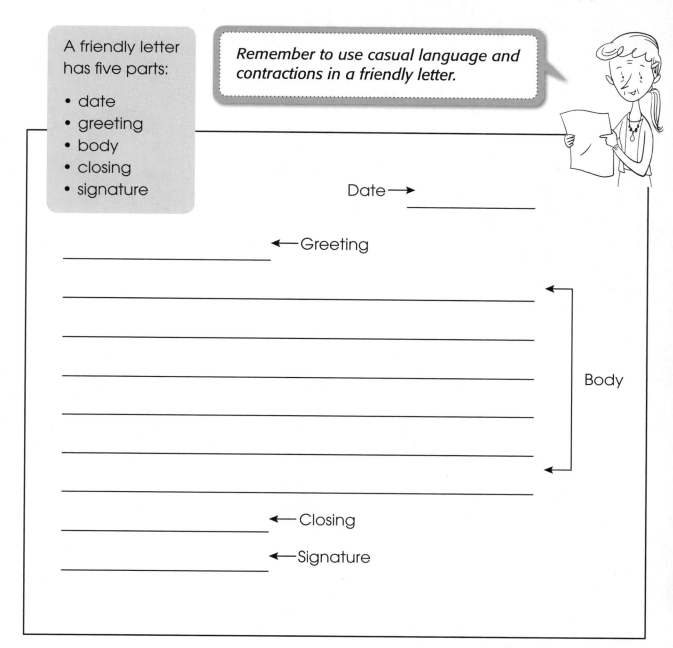

A friendly letter has five parts:

- date
- greeting
- body
- closing
- signature

Remember to use casual language and contractions in a friendly letter.

Date →

←Greeting

Body

←Closing

←Signature

Words that I Have Learned

UNIT 2 Camp Wannastay

Friday, July 10

Dear Diary,

Saying goodbye to Mom, Dad, and Erica was a breeze. I imagined a whole week without my little sister pestering me would be like heaven, but now, I'm feeling differently. It's the end of my first day at camp and I'm dreading the remainder of the week. I thought I was ready for overnight camp, but I guess I'm not.

Dear Diary,

Saturday, July 11

Today, camp went a lot better than I anticipated. Steve, the camp counsellor, is absolutely the coolest. He organized cooperative games so the campers could get to know one another. We also went canoeing and I was paired up with a quiet guy named Shawn. I initiated conversation with him and he became more at ease. Canoeing was a blast! I think we frightened away all the wildlife with the ruckus we created during the splash fight with our paddles. I got totally drenched!

Dear Diary,

Sunday, July 12

Today was a great bonding experience for the guys in our cabin. The counsellor arranged a competition among the cabins. We came in fourth place in the scavenger hunt, narrowly missing third. The lake water was frigid for the swimming relay, but we placed second regardless. The final event worth the most points was the obstacle course. It was quite challenging, but we had an awesome time. We put forth our finest effort and it paid off – first place for our team! I can honestly say, the feeling of homesickness has completely diminished.

A.   Circle the answers.

1.   Who is writing the diary
     entries?

     Shawn

     Erica

     unknown

2.   Who is described as
     being "absolutely the
     coolest"?

     Steve

     Shawn

     Eric

3.   How long will the writer be
     staying at Camp Wannastay?

     three days

     one week

     three weeks

4.   What place does the writer's
     team come in for the obstacle
     course competition?

     first place

     second place

     fourth place

B.   Answer the questions.

1.   What text form is "Camp Wannastay"?

     _____

2.   What are some features of this text form?

     _____

     _____

3.   Why does the writer think that the camp counsellor is the
     coolest?

     _____

     _____

     _____

Section
4

Reading and Writing

A diary is a written record of a person's feelings and experiences on a daily basis. It is written in the first person because the writer is writing about himself/herself. It is mostly in the past tense as it describes events that happened. The writing in a diary is usually informal because it is a record of private thoughts.

C. **Imagine that you are a camper at Camp Wannastay. Plan what you will write in your diary after your fourth day at the camp.**

EVENTS Describe the events of the day.

 Where did you go?

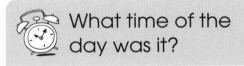 What time of the day was it?

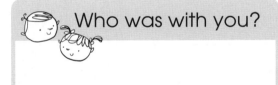 Who was with you?

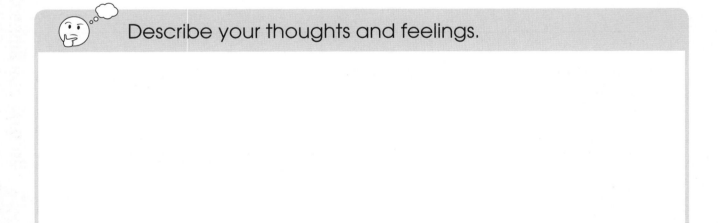 Describe your thoughts and feelings.

D. Write a diary entry for your fourth day at Camp Wannastay using your plan from (C).

_____

_____

_____

_____

_____

_____

_____

_____

_____

_____

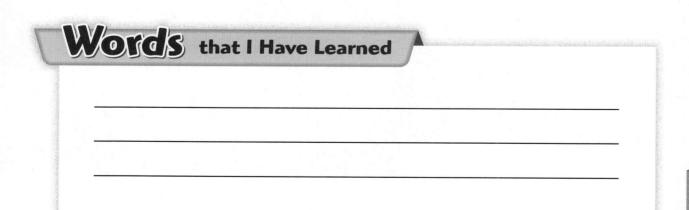

Words that I Have Learned

_____

_____

_____

UNIT 3

The Father, the Son, and the Donkey

One day, a man set off with his son to the market to sell their donkey. As they were walking with the donkey by their side, a passer-by said to the man, "Hey, how come you have a donkey but you don't ride on it?" Upon hearing that, the man climbed onto the donkey and rode on it. "Yes, he's right. It's less tiring this way," he thought.

Soon a woman passed by and said, "What's the matter with you? You have your boy walk and you sit comfortably on the donkey?" Upon hearing that, the man quickly got off and put his son on the donkey. "Yes, I think she's right. I should let my son ride on the donkey instead of me."

They had not gone far when an old man yelled at the man's son, "Hey, you should get off and let your father ride the donkey! You're young and full of energy." Confused, the man decided to climb onto the donkey and ride on it together with his son.

The donkey trudged along slowly, huffing and puffing. As they passed by a crowd, a few people jeered at them. One of them pointed to the donkey and said, "Look at your donkey! How do you expect it to carry both of you?"

"Well, I think they're right. We're too heavy for the donkey," the man thought. So he and his son got off and pondered what they should do. Then they got hold of a pole and some strings. They tied the donkey's feet to the pole and started carrying the donkey together.

"It's heavy, but at least no one would say we're wrong," said the man to his son.

When they reached a narrow bridge, the donkey managed to get one of its legs loose and kicked frantically. Losing balance, the three fell off the bridge and into the water!

In trying to please everyone, the man ended up pleasing no one and got himself into trouble.

A. Circle the answers.

1. Why is the man taking his donkey to the market?

   to sell it

   to give it exercise

   to buy food for it

2. Who rides the donkey at the beginning of the story?

   the man

   his son

   no one

3. Who thinks that the boy should ride the donkey?

   the boy

   a woman

   an old man

4. What do they use to carry the donkey?

   a wagon

   a wheelbarrow

   a pole and some strings

B. Answer the questions.

This story is a fable. A fable is a short story that teaches a moral or a lesson. The moral usually comes at the end of the fable.

1. Why does the crowd jeer at the man and his son?

   _____

   _____

2. What is the problem in this story?

   _____

   _____

3. What is the moral of this fable?

   _____

   _____

C. **Plan your own fable with the story planner.**

 Besides teaching a moral lesson, a fable consists of all the elements below as a story does. It is also common for a fable to include talking animals as characters.

Title: _____

Characters (Who?)

Events (What happens?)

Setting (Where? When?)

Problem ??

Solution

Moral

_____

_____

_____

_____

D. **Write a fable using your ideas from (C).**

Title: _____

_____

_____

_____

_____

_____

_____

_____

_____

_____

_____

_____

Words that I Have Learned

_____

_____

_____

UNIT 4

A Pet's Tale

The pet store was full of pets to adopt.

I was the lucky one that day, I thought.

Cuddled in her arms, freed from that store.

Onto new adventures and much, much more.

Romping in the backyard, chewing a bone.

Life was marvellous, I no longer felt alone.

But then after months, it seemed nobody cared.

The responsibility and commitment was not shared.

The girl got busy with friends and homework, you see.

And I was stuck in a cage again, and wanted to be free.

One day I heard the mom argue with her daughter.

Constant reminding of my walk, food, and water.

She said I'd have to be sent to another owner.

Someone not so busy; I wouldn't have to be a loner.

My happiness there was coming to an end.

How would my broken heart ever mend?

But call it a miracle or fortune, it matters not.

It was a wonderful home where I was brought.

The lady was retired and lived on her own.

She longed for a companion; didn't want to be alone.

We were an instant match for each other.

The good times we had – like child and mother.

You'd think I was royalty – always treated like a queen.

Our affection for each other was always seen.

A. Circle the answers.

1. Who is telling the story?

   a cat

   a dog

   a hamster

2. Where is the pet at the beginning?

   in a park

   in an animal shelter

   in a pet store

3. Why does the girl stop caring for her pet?

   She wants another pet.

   She is lazy.

   She is busy.

4. Who is the pet's new owner?

   the girl

   the girl's mother

   a retired lady

B. Answer the questions.

1. In the first stanza, why does the pet think it is lucky?

   _____

   _____

2. How does the new owner treat the pet?

A poem consists of stanzas, which are like paragraphs in a written text, with each having its own theme.

The tone is the writer's attitude or feeling about a topic. It can be happy, sad, humorous, etc.

   _____

   _____

3. What is the writer's tone in each stanza of the poem?

   1st Stanza _____   2nd Stanza _____

   3rd Stanza _____   4th Stanza _____

C. Read "A Pet's Tale" again. Then write the words that rhyme with the words below.

1. store _____

2. alone _____

3. cared _____

4. see _____

 Some poems rhyme. Rhyming words do not have to be spelled with the same ending or have the same number of syllables.

5. water _____

6. loner _____

7. end _____

8. own _____

9. mother _____

10. seen _____

D. Fill in the blanks with the correct words to complete the rhyming poem.

 This poem follows an AABB rhyme scheme, that is, the first and the second lines rhyme, and the third and the fourth lines rhyme.

| sleep   night   bright   cheep |

In the Morning

The morning sun shines _____ .

Days replace the _____ .

Flowers awake from their _____ .

Birds sing cheep, _____ .

E. Write a two-stanza poem using the AABB rhyme scheme. Give your poem a title. Then draw a picture to go with it.

Title: _____

A _____

A _____

B _____

B _____

A _____

A _____

B _____

B _____

Topic Ideas
- The Storm
- The Cuddly Cat
- A Starry Night
- My Best Friend
- The Haunted House

Words that I Have Learned

_____

_____

_____

UNIT 5

A Rebus Invitation

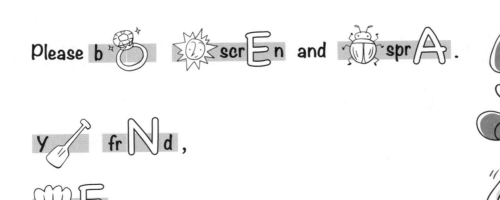

A. Circle the answers.

1. What is the invitation for?

   a birthday party

   a wedding

   a family gathering

2. When does the party start?

   in the morning

   in the afternoon

   in the evening

3. Where will the party take place?

   outdoors

   indoors

   on a cruise ship

4. What will be served at the party?

   breakfast

   lunch

   dinner

B. Answer the questions.

1. How is this a rebus? Give two examples.

    Rebus uses a combination of letters, pictures, symbols, and words to represent a word or a phrase.

   _____

   _____

   Examples: _____

   _____

2. What are the paragraphs in the rebus about?

   Paragraph 1: _____

   Paragraph 2: _____

   Paragraph 3: _____

3. What does the guest need to bring?

   _____

C. **Read "A Rebus Invitation" again. Then rewrite the invitation without using rebus.**

An Invitation

_____ ,

_____

_____

_____

_____

_____

_____

_____ ,

_____

D. **Pretend that you are inviting a friend to your birthday party. Plan what you will write in your rebus invitation.**

Date:

Time:

Location:

Guest's Name:

Food and Drinks:

Activities:

E. Write a rebus invitation using your ideas from (D).

An Invitation

Remember to use letters, pictures, symbols, and words.

Words that I Have Learned

_____

_____

_____

UNIT 6
New France – the Beginning of Canada

Before 1500
- Various indigenous communities were located across the area of present-day Quebec.

1497
- John Cabot, an Englishman, reached Canada.

1534
- The French, who were in competition with the English, decided to explore North America. Francis I, king of France, selected Jacques Cartier to lead a voyage. Cartier reached what is now Newfoundland and explored New Brunswick and Prince Edward Island. He claimed the land for France.

1535
- Cartier set off on his second voyage. He was led to the St. Lawrence River and reached what is now Montreal. He came upon impassable rapids and was forced to spend the winter there.

1541
- Cartier set sail on his third voyage. He established a settlement at present-day Quebec City and tried to find the rich kingdom of Saguenay. He failed to do so and suffered hardship and illness through the winter. Cartier abandoned the settlement in the spring after a harsh winter and an attack from indigenous peoples.

1608
- Samuel de Champlain established a settlement in Quebec City that became the beginning of the development of Canada as a nation. French settlements sprang up along the St. Lawrence River. New France developed and was firmly established by the end of the 17th century.

1759
- The English and the French fought over this new territory. The historic battle on the Plains of Abraham occurred in Quebec City. The English, led by General Wolfe, defeated Montcalm and the French.

1763–1774
- The Royal Proclamation of 1763 and the Quebec Act of 1774 allowed the French to maintain their culture, religion, traditions, and language in Quebec under British rule.

A. Circle the answers.

1. Whom did Francis I, king of France, select to lead the first voyage?

   John Cabot

   Jacques Cartier

   Samuel de Champlain

2. Where did Jacques Cartier spend the winter in 1535?

   near the St. Lawrence River

   in Montreal

   in Quebec City

3. Where did Samuel de Champlain establish a settlement in 1608?

   in Quebec City

   in Montreal

   in Ottawa

4. In what year was the Quebec Act signed?

   in 1763

   in 1774

   in 1759

B. Answer the questions.

1. Why is it useful to present history in a timeline?

    A timeline is a graphic line that shows a list of events in the order that they happened.

   _____

   _____

2. Why did the English and the French fight in 1759?

   _____

   _____

3. What did the Royal Proclamation and the Quebec Act allow the French to maintain?

   _____

   _____

C. Plan your own timeline by completing the chart.

Suggested Topics

- The Building of the Great Wall of China
- The Evolution of Computers
- The History of the Olympics
- The History of Space Travel
- My Family History

You can research one of the suggested topics or come up with your own topic.

My Topic

	Date or Year	Important Event
1		
2		
3		
4		
5		
6		

D. **Create a timeline using your ideas from (C). Add pictures wherever possible.**

Title: _____

Date/Year

_____

_____

_____

_____

_____

_____

_____

_____

Words that I Have Learned

_____

_____

_____

UNIT 7

Seal Island

Amazing Seal Island

Great White Shark

Cape Fur Seal

See the seals,
See the sharks,
See South Africa!

Where

Seal Island is about 5 km off shore in False Bay, South Africa.

Seal Island

What

Seal Island is a small rocky island, home to approximately 64 000 Cape Fur Seals! You can also see Great White Sharks!

When

The best time to see Great White Sharks is from February to September.

Weather

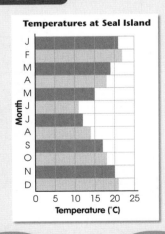

Temperatures at Seal Island

Month: J F M A M J J A S O N D
Temperature (°C): 0 5 10 15 20 25

How

Catch a boat to Seal Island!

Seals in the sun

Interesting Facts about the Cape Fur Seal and the Great White Shark

- The seal feeds on crabs, squid, and schools of fish.
- The shark feeds on fish and seals.
- In the cooler months from April to September, the seal becomes the shark's main meal as the fish that the shark usually forages on migrate.
- There is a quick drop in the depth of water from the island where the shark hides and ambushes its prey.
- The shark, camouflaged by the dark, rocky bottom of the sea, ambushes the seal and then breaches and strikes the seal.
- This area surrounding Seal Island has fittingly been named the "ring of peril" for the seal because it risks its life each time it leaves the island to find food.

Seal Island Adventures

Seal Island Adventures

sealislandadventures@pop.com
123-456-7891

Book a trip now!

For more information, visit www.si-a.com.

A. Circle the answers.

1. Where is Seal Island?

   in the South Pole

   in South America

   in South Africa

2. What is the best time to see the Great White Shark?

   from January to June

   from February to September

   from September to February

3. How do you get to Seal Island?

   by plane

   by boat

   on foot

4. What do seals eat?

   squid, fish, and sharks

   seals, sharks, and fish

   crabs, squid, and fish

B. Answer the questions.

1. Is this text a brochure? How?

   _____

   _____

   _____

 A brochure is a piece of folded paper that is intended to spread information and/or promote a product, service, business, etc.

2. From whom is this text?

   _____

3. How do Great White Sharks hunt seals for food?

   _____

   _____

4. What is "the ring of peril"?

   _____

   _____

C.   Read "Seal Island" again. Then fill in the answers.

1.   Title: _____

2.   Slogan: _____

         _____

         _____

A brochure has these features. It may also have subheadings and text boxes.

3.   Headings: _____

         _____

4.   Images: _____

5.   Caption: _____

6.   Company: _____

7.   Contact: _____

8.   Website: _____

D.   Brainstorm ideas for a brochure that you will create.

You can promote a product or a service with your brochure.

Ideas for My Brochure

E. **Create a brochure using your ideas from (D).**

front panel

Words that I Have Learned

_____

_____

_____

UNIT 8

The Production of Milk

Milk Production Process

Dairy cows graze on pastures on a dairy farm.

pasture

The cows are milked twice a day. In the past, farmers milked cows by hand. Nowadays, most dairy farms use milking machines.

milking machine

tanker

The milk is transported to a processing factory by well-insulated refrigerated tankers to keep the milk cold.

silos

The milk is stored in refrigerated silos at a temperature below 4°C for no more than 48 hours.

processing factory

On arriving at the factory, the milk is stored in refrigerated silos first. Then it is pasteurized and homogenized.

packaging machine

The processed milk is transported through pipes to automatic packaging machines where it is packaged.

refrigerated room

The packaged milk is stored in a large refrigerated room before being delivered to stores.

A. Circle the answers.

1. How many times are cows milked a day?

   one time

   two times

   four times

2. What temperature should milk be stored in the silos?

   above 4°C

   below 4°C

   at 4°C

3. How is processed milk packaged?

   by hand

   by manual packaging machines

   by automatic packaging machines

4. Where is the milk stored after packaging?

   in refrigerated silos

   in refrigerated tankers

   in refrigerated rooms

B. Answer the questions.

1. What does the diagram show?

   _____

   _____

    A flow diagram is a diagram that shows the sequence, stages, or steps of a process. It may contain pictures or only text.

2. What is the difference between milking cows in the past and milking cows in the present?

   _____

   _____

3. How is milk processed in a processing factory?

   _____

   _____

C. **Read "The Production of Milk" again. Then fill in and circle the answers.**

1. Title: _____

2. Labels: _____

_____

_____

_____

_____

_____

_____

Apart from these features, a flow diagram contains arrows and lines to show the direction of flow. Some have brief descriptions of each stage in the process.

3. Images: boxes / illustrations / symbols

D. **Brainstorm and research ideas for a flow diagram that you will create.**

You can also come up with your own topic.

Topic Ideas

- Planning a Birthday Party
- How to Make a Scrapbook
- The Recycling Process
- Preparing for an Outing

E. Create a flow diagram using your ideas from (D). Include as many of the features as possible.

Title

Words that I Have Learned

_____

_____

_____

UNIT
9 Salamanders

Salamanders

A salamander is an amphibian whose long body is roundish in the centre and includes four limbs and a tail. Its eyes are round with eyelids, but it has neither eardrums nor claws. The majority of the 356 species of salamanders in the world live in warm climates.

Although most salamanders have common features, there are distinct differences from one species to another. The red salamander, for example, has no lungs and breathes through its skin, which must always be moist. This means that its habitat must be on riverbanks or in wet forests. These forest dwellers lay eggs from which miniature salamanders emerge, without passing through the larval stage.

The Mud Puppy

The "Mud Puppy" is actually one of the 19 species of salamanders in Canada. The Mud Puppy, which is distinct because of the three pairs of red gills on each side of its head, lives its entire life in the water. Other species of salamanders spend only part of their time in the water.

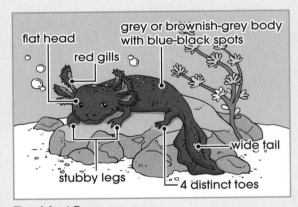

The Mud Puppy

The Life Cycle

In spring, most salamanders migrate to ponds where they reproduce. The eggs are deposited in the water in little bundles or larger oval masses. The larvae, like the adults, feed on other animals. The metamorphosis of the salamander is usually completed by the end of summer. This is very much unlike its cousin, the frog, whose transformation from egg to adult is very gradual.

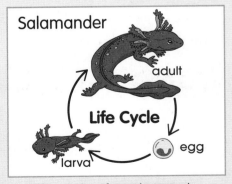

The life cycle of a salamander

A. Circle the answers.

1. What is a salamander?

    a mammal

    an amphibian

    a reptile

2. Most salamanders live in
    _____ .

    cold climates

    hot climates

    warm climates

3. How do red salamanders breathe?

    with their lungs

    through their skin

    through their feet

4. How many salamander species are there in Canada?

    19

    356

    4

B. Answer the questions.

1. What is the topic of this textbook entry?

    _____

 A textbook is a book with information on a particular subject.

2. What are some physical features of a salamander?

    _____

3. How is the Mud Puppy different from other salamanders?

    _____

    _____

4. Describe the life cycle of a salamander.

    _____

    _____

Section

4

Reading and Writing

C. **Read "Salamanders" again. Then fill in the answers.**

1. Title: _____

2. Heading: _____

3. Subheadings: _____

   _____

 The features of a textbook entry include a title, headings, subheadings, photographs and/or illustrations, and graphs, diagrams, or charts including labels and captions.

4. What types of images are used in the passage?

_____

_____

D. **Brainstorm ideas for a textbook entry that you will write.**

 **My Ideas**

E. Write a textbook entry using your ideas from (D). Then draw a picture and add a caption to go with your entry.

UNIT

← Title

Picture

← Heading

← Subheading

Caption

Words that I Have Learned

UNIT 10

Disasters at Sea

Disasters at Sea

While the sinking of the Titanic is the most notorious shipwreck of all time, there are numerous other marine tragedies. The sinking of the Empress of Ireland and the Lusitania are other notable disasters at sea.

The Titanic

On April 10, 1912, the Titanic departed on her maiden voyage from Southampton, England heading across the Atlantic to New York City. Four days after leaving Southampton, a lookout spotted an iceberg approaching out of the fog. A minute later, the iceberg struck the hull

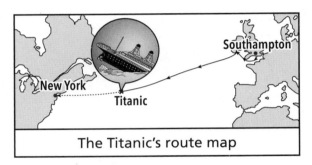

The Titanic's route map

of the Titanic causing severe damage. In less than three hours, the ship split in two and the bow plunged into the sea. The ship was not equipped with enough lifeboats to carry all the passengers. Many passengers were left helplessly floating in the dark, cold waters of the Atlantic. Over 1500 people died that fateful night.

The Empress of Ireland

Just two years after the Titanic tragedy, the Empress of Ireland, another upscale passenger ship, sank in the St. Lawrence River just east of Quebec City. In the early morning of May 30, 1914, a Norwegian coal ship, the Storstad, rammed the Empress of Ireland in thick fog. It took only 14 minutes for the liner to sink. Of the 1477 passengers on board, 1012 died.

The Lusitania

Three years after the Titanic tragedy, the Lusitania met the same fate. The Lusitania transported passengers from North America to Ireland. In 1914, a war broke out between the British and the Germans and on May 7, 1915, a German submarine torpedoed the Lusitania off the southern coast of Ireland. The ship sank completely in 18 minutes. Of the 1959 people on board, 1195 lost their lives.

The Lusitania before sinking

The Titanic, the Empress of Ireland, and the Lusitania were all closely related in structure. Sadly, they all suffered the same fate.

A. Circle the answers.

1. In which year did the Titanic sink?

   in 1912

   in 1914

   in 1915

2. Where was the Titanic heading?

   to Southampton

   to Atlantic City

   to New York City

3. How many passengers were on board the Empress of Ireland?

   1477

   1500

   1959

4. Which ship sank off the southern coast of Ireland?

   the Titanic

   the Empress of Ireland

   the Lusitania

B. Answer the questions.

1. How is this text non-fiction?

   _____

   _____

 Non-fiction is informational texts that are true stories based on facts and real life.

2. Briefly describe how the three ships sank.

   The Titanic: _____

   _____

   The Empress of Ireland: _____

   _____

   The Lusitania: _____

   _____

C. **Read "Disasters at Sea" again. Then fill in and circle the answers.**

1. Title: _____

2. Headings: _____

    _____

    _____

 Informational texts can have the following structures: problem and solution, cause and effect, compare and contrast, description or list, and time order or sequence.

3. Images: photo / picture / graph / diagram / map

4. Captions: _____ , _____

5. Structure: _____

    _____

6. Assume this is an informational text in a non-fiction book. Give a title to the book.

    _____

D. **Brainstorm and research ideas for another informational text for the non-fiction book in Question 6 in (C).**

 My Ideas

E. Write an informational text for a non-fiction book using your ideas from (D). Then draw a picture and add a caption to go with the text.

_____ ← Book Title

_____ ← Title of the Text

_____

_____

_____

_____

_____

_____

_____

_____

_____

Caption → _____

Words that I Have Learned

_____

_____

_____

UNIT 11 The Case of the Disappearing Fish

THE SMART DAILY NEWS

August 14, 2019

Prized Pet Fish Missing from Backyard Pond

By Percival O'Brien

The pond in José's backyard, where three fish have gone missing

Early Saturday morning, a boy named José reported that one of his prized pet fish had gone missing under suspicious circumstances. Then on Sunday, he reported another fish missing, and another on Monday.

José lives in the suburbs near Rattray Marsh and is very proud of his backyard which has a garden and a pond with a beautiful waterfall. He claims that he has worked hard to ensure that his backyard is a suitable and healthy environment for his pet fish and frogs. In his report, José claimed that he was "devastated and confused" by the loss of his three fish.

José believed that there were three possible suspects who may have stolen his fish: two of his neighbours and a suspicious cat that he had seen walking across the fence of his backyard. One neighbour is an animal lover who believes that animals should not be kept in captivity. José claimed that she had often threatened

to release his fish and frogs into a natural habitat. The other neighbour loves fish and frogs, especially when they are breaded and deep-fried. He often teased José about sneaking into his backyard to catch a delicious seafood meal.

As it turns out, the thief was not one of José's suspects; it was actually a large bird that had been swooping down into his backyard to take fish from his pond. José discovered the bird when he was hiding behind a bush in his backyard one night to catch the thief. By sunrise, he had almost given up when he saw the creature swoop down and fly over the top of his head. José described the sighting, "When I saw the size of the bird, my eyes widened in disbelief. I cannot believe that I was completely wrong the entire time."

A. Circle the answers.

1. How many fish have disappeared?

   one

   two

   three

2. Where does José live?

   in the city

   in the suburbs

   in the countryside

3. Where does José keep his fish?

   in Rattray Marsh

   in his pond

   behind a bush

4. How does José feel about losing his fish?

   prized

   proud

   devastated

B. Answer the questions.

1. What is the topic of this newspaper article?

   _____

 A newspaper article is a written report on a specific topic; it is often news on a current event.

2. Describe José's backyard.

   _____

3. Why were José's two neighbours possible suspects?

   _____

   _____

   _____

4. Who was the thief?

   _____

Section
4

Reading and Writing

C. **Read "The Case of the Disappearing Fish" again. Then fill in and circle the answers.**

1.　Date: _____

2.　Headline: _____

3.　Byline: _____

A newspaper article contains all these features. The body gives details about the topic (who, what, when, where, why, and how).

4.　Introduction:　Paragraph(s)　1　2　3　4

5.　Body:　Paragraph(s)　1　2　3　4

6.　Quotes: _____

_____

_____

7.　Caption: _____

D. **Brainstorm ideas for a newspaper article that you will write.**

Who

What

Where

Why

How

When

E. Write a newspaper article using your ideas from (D). Then draw a photo and add a caption to go with the article.

THE SMART DAILY NEWS _____ ← Date

_____ ← Headline

_____ ← Byline

_____   _____

_____   _____

_____   _____

_____   _____

_____

_____

_____

_____   ↑
                            Caption

Words that I Have Learned

_____

_____

_____

UNIT 12

Being the Eldest

	From:	evan_s@pop.com
	To:	kidsadvicemagazine@pop.com
Send	Subject:	Advice for My Sibling Situation

Dear Kids Advice Magazine:

My name is Evan and being the eldest child in the family surely has its disadvantages. First of all, I have to share all my toys and games with my younger siblings, Julia and William. Of course, they do not need to return the favour because I am totally uninterested in their things. Besides that, Julia and William are always hanging around me. It is especially irritating when I have a friend over. We look for a secluded place in the house where they cannot disturb us, but within minutes, they have found us and are asking to join in. I just cannot seem to get a moment's peace.

At mealtimes, I have to eat whatever is on my plate regardless of the portion size or taste. Julia and William only need to try one bite when it is not their favourite food. Not only this, but I am expected to be cooperative at all times just because I am the eldest and need to be a role model for them.

It does not seem fair either that I have more chores to do around the house than Julia and William put together. Moreover, when it comes to practising our musical instruments, I have to practise more than double the time. Oh, and the worst part of it all is the huge quantities of homework I get compared to them.

I am feeling rather annoyed with my sibling situation. Can you please write back with some advice?

Yours truly,
Evan Smith

A. Circle the answers.

1. Who is the sender of this e-mail?

   Kids Advice Magazine

   Julia and William

   Evan Smith

2. Who is the recipient?

   Kids Advice Magazine

   Julia and William

   Evan Smith

3. Who is the eldest sibling?

   Julia

   William

   Evan

4. What does Evan not like to share?

   his toys

   his food

   his musical instruments

B. Answer the questions.

1. Is this e-mail formal or informal? Why?

   _____

   _____

E-mail stands for electronic mail, which is a letter sent through the Internet. E-mails can be formal (for business purposes) or informal (for family and friends).

2. What is the subject of this e-mail?

   _____

3. What is the purpose of this e-mail?

   _____

4. Why is Evan annoyed with his siblings? Give two reasons.

   Reason 1: _____

   _____

   Reason 2: _____

   _____

C. Label the features of the e-mail.

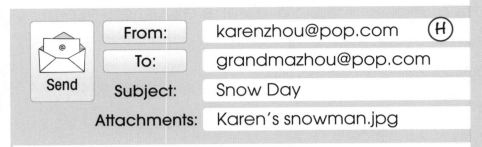

From:	karenzhou@pop.com	Ⓗ
To:	grandmazhou@pop.com
Subject:	Snow Day
Attachments:	Karen's snowman.jpg

Send

Ⓐ sender
Ⓑ subject
Ⓒ body
Ⓓ closing
Ⓔ attachment
Ⓕ recipient
Ⓖ salutation
Ⓗ sender's e-mail address
Ⓘ recipient's e-mail address

Hey Grandma,

How are you? It's snowing here right now. It's so cold! We had a snowstorm and we got to stay at home instead of going to school. I made a snowman. He has a carrot for a nose and blueberries for eyes. I took a picture for you!

Miss you tons,
Karen

Karen's snowman.jpg

D. Imagine that you are Karen's Grandma. Brainstorm ideas for a reply e-mail to Karen.

My Ideas

E. **Write a reply e-mail using your ideas from (D).**

From:

To:

Send Subject:

_____

_____

_____

_____

_____

_____

_____

_____

_____

_____

_____

_____

Should this e-mail be formal or informal? What language should you use?

Words that I Have Learned

_____

_____

_____

13 Nature's Fireworks

aurora borealis

aurora borealis – Aurora borealis (Latin for "dawn of the North") is a scientific term for the natural light phenomenon that appears in the sky in the Northern Hemisphere. It is often called the northern lights. In the Southern Hemisphere, this natural phenomenon is called aurora australis, or the southern lights. The northern and southern auroras usually appear as mirror-like images at the same time in many shapes and vivid colours.

Aurora borealis in Whitehorse, Yukon, Canada

Auroras are caused by particles that are shot out into space by the sun. When these particles reach Earth, they are drawn into the magnetic field that surrounds Earth. When these particles collide with different gases in our atmosphere, auroras are produced. Since the magnetic field is strongest in the North, that is where auroras are often spotted.

Myths and Legends

For thousands of years, there were many myths and legends that people told to explain this phenomenon.

• The Inuit of Alaska believed that the lights were the spirits of the animals they hunted – seals, salmon, deer, and beluga whales.

• The Menominee of Wisconsin regarded the lights as torches used by great, friendly giants in the North to help them spear fish at night.

• Other Aboriginal peoples believed that the lights were the spirits of their people, and some an omen of war.

A. Circle the answers.

1. What language is "aurora borealis" in?

    French

    Greek

    Latin

2. What is aurora borealis?

    Earth's magnetic field

    one of Earth's hemispheres

    a natural light phenomenon

3. What is another name for aurora australis?

    the northern lights

    the southern lights

    dawn of the North

4. Where is Earth's magnetic field strongest?

    in the North

    in the South

    at the equator

B. Answer the questions.

1. What is the topic of this encyclopedia entry?

    _____

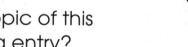 An encyclopedia is a book or a set of books consisting of entries put in alphabetical order that provides detailed explanations on many topics.

2. How are auroras created?

    _____

    _____

3. How did people from long ago explain the northern lights?

    The Inuit of Alaska: _____

    _____

    The Menominee of Wisconsin: _____

    _____

    Other Aboriginal peoples: _____

    _____

C.   Read "Nature's Fireworks" again. Then fill in and circle the answers.

1.   Entry: _____

2.   Subheading: _____

3.   Image: photo / diagram / graph / chart

4.   Caption: _____

_____

Apart from these features, an encyclopedia often includes a table of contents, an index, and a glossary.

D.   Brainstorm and research ideas for another encyclopedia entry that you will write.

You can research one of the suggested topics or come up with your own topic.

Suggested Topics

• mammal
• compass
• town
• GPS
• cheese
• board game
• tornado
• air pollution

My Ideas

E. Create an encyclopedia entry using your ideas from (D). Include an image and a caption.

↳ Heading

_____ – ← Entry

↳ Caption

Words that I Have Learned

UNIT 14 Stonehenge

www.stonehenge.pop.com

Stonehenge Uncovered

Stonehenge Uncovered

Home | Visit | Learn | Contact

Search

Learn

Watch a tour of Stonehenge.

Stonehenge

Stonehenge is one of the world's most well-known monuments. We know many incredible things about it. But, built around 5000 years ago, Stonehenge is most famous for what we do not know about it.

Stonehenge in Wiltshire, England

What is it?

Stonehenge is a formation of large stones arranged in a ring, with most standing on end. The largest of the stones are the sarsen stones in the outer ring. They are nearly three stories tall, each weighing more than three African elephants.

What we do not know is what Stonehenge was used for. Was it a place of worship or a place to observe stars? Was it a calendar or a burial ground? There is some evidence of all these, but we may never know for sure. The size of Stonehenge is also the cause of one of its biggest mysteries. Who built it? How did they erect the stones and lay the stone lintels on top?

What happens twice a year?

The stones of Stonehenge are mathematically arranged to line up with the sunrise during the summer solstice. On the morning of the longest day of the year, the sun shines directly through its entrance. And in the evening of the year's shortest day, it does the same.

Is it a coincidence? If it was deliberately built to align with the solstice sun, why?

A. Circle the answers.

1. When was Stonehenge built?

   around 5000 BCE

   around 5000 CE

   around 5000 years ago

2. Which one is not a mystery about Stonehenge?

   what it was used for

   how it was built

   where it was built

3. What are the stones in the outer ring called?

   ring stones

   sarsen stones

   lintels

4. What are the stones on top called?

   sarsen stones

   lintels

   top stones

B. Answer the questions.

1. What is the purpose of this website?

   _____

   _____

A website is a source of information on the Internet. Different websites have different purposes, such as e-commerce (for business) and social networking/media (for connecting people).

2. What is Stonehenge?

   _____

3. Describe the sarsen stones.

   _____

   _____

4. How are the stones of Stonehenge mathematically arranged?

   _____

   _____

C.   **Read "Stonehenge" again. Then fill in and check the answers.**

1.   Heading: _____

2.   Subheadings: _____

3.   Image: _____

4.   Caption: _____

5.   What other features does the website have?

     ◯ links   ◯ lists

     ◯ search box   ◯ footer

     ◯ main menu bar

     ◯ paragraphs

     ◯ navigation buttons

     ◯ audio or video

6.   What does the footer contain?

     ◯ site map

     ◯ contact information

     ◯ copyright symbol with year

     ◯ privacy policy

     ◯ terms of use

     ◯ social media links

D.   **Brainstorm ideas for a website that you will create.**

My Ideas

_____

E. **Create a website using your ideas from (D).**

Words that I Have Learned

_____

_____

_____

Section 4

Reading and Writing

A. Circle the answers.

1. What are some features of a letter?

    pictures, signature, subject

    date, greeting, signature

    stanzas, date, greeting

2. How are diary entries organized?

    in alphabetical order

    in chronological order

    in random order

3. The moral of a fable can be found _____ of the fable.

    at the beginning

    in the middle

    at the end

4. What can a fable have as characters?

    real people

    talking animals

    celebrities

5. Stanzas in a poem are like _____ in a written text.

    headlines

    captions

    paragraphs

6. Which follows the AABB scheme?

    raw, king, sing, saw

    hair, map, chair, clap

    late, fate, bell, spell

7. What is this?

    a rebus

    a caption

    a flow diagram

8. Which is an example of a timeline?

9. What does a brochure do?

    warns people

    advertises products

    entertains readers

10. What is this brochure promoting?

a vacation

a cooking course

rental homes

11. What type of text is this?

a flow diagram

a timeline

a non-fiction text

12. What is the purpose of a History textbook?

to make a request

to communicate

to provide information

13. The "_____" symbol is placed in an e-mail address.

$

@

%

14. An encyclopedia is _____ .

a media text

a literary text

an informational text

15. What does Ⓐ represent?

a caption

the date

a quote

16. What type of text is this?

Birth   **1st Birthday**   **School**

a timeline

a letter

a brochure

17. Which can be used to write about feelings?

a non-fiction text

a diary

an encyclopedia

B.   Read the text. Then write "T" for the true statements and "F" for the false ones.

THE SMART DAILY NEWS

August 28, 1956

Paricutín Volcano – from Cornfield to Volcano

By Julie García

While visiting the Mexican site of the Paricutín volcano at San Salvador Paricutín on Tuesday, Canadian geologist Ross Green said, "It is a rare and great opportunity to be able to study the birth, growth, and death of a volcano." It has been reported that it all started when a farmer, standing in the middle of a cornfield in 1943, heard a rumbling sound beneath. To his astonishment, he saw the ground crack open and bulge to about two metres high. Smoke and ash began to spew into the air, followed by a loud whistling sound. Fearing the worst, the farmer fled the scene and returned the next day to find that the swelling of the earth had grown to a height of nine metres and was forcefully flinging out rocks. By the end of the day, it had grown another 36 metres. The farmer had just witnessed the birth of a volcano. Throughout the night, lava shot up over 300 metres and spread rapidly over the cornfield.

This powerful explosive period continued for a year where the cone of the volcano reached a height of 336 metres. The cone continued to grow for eight more years, reaching a final height of 424 metres. Six months before the volcano died, it had its most violent activity. By the end, over 900 million tons of lava had destroyed San Salvador Paricutín

Canadian geologist Ross Green near the church in San Juan

and the neighbouring village of San Juan, and volcanic ash had choked surrounding forests.

Of all the things in the two villages, only one building survived this monstrous volcano. Today, surrounded by hardened lava, the remains of a church in the village of San Juan can still be seen – a desolate reminder of the ferocious event.

1. In 1943, a volcano emerged in San Salvador Paricutín, Mexico. _____

2. The volcano reached a final height of 424 metres. _____

3. Over 90 million tons of lava destroyed the two villages. _____

4. The explosion occurred six months before the volcano died. _____

5. The only building that survived was a church. _____

C.   Answer the questions.

1. What type of text is this? List two text features.

   _____

   Features: _____ , _____

2. Explain how the cornfield turned into a volcano.

   _____

   _____

3. What does the "death" of a volcano mean?

   _____

4. Why does the Canadian geologist Ross Green say that the volcano is an opportunity?

   _____

5. Describe the landscape after the volcanic eruption.

   _____

6. Suggest a way to ensure that people are protected during a volcanic eruption.

   _____

D.   Write and draw to complete the flow diagram.

Steps to Making a Volcano at Home

Have a parent supervise you. Step back when the "volcano" erupts.

Step 1

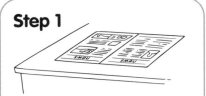

Prepare your work surface by laying down some newspaper.

Step 2

Place a jar in the centre of the newspaper.

Step 5

Pour two teaspoons of baking soda into the "volcano".

Step 6

Pour 1 cup of vinegar into the "volcano".

Step 3

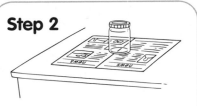

_____

_____

_____

_____

Step 7

Now step back. The volcano

_____ .

Step 4

dishwashing liquid

_____

_____

_____

food colouring

E. **Create a website to promote tourism in San Salvador Paricutín and San Juan. Draw pictures and add captions for your website.**

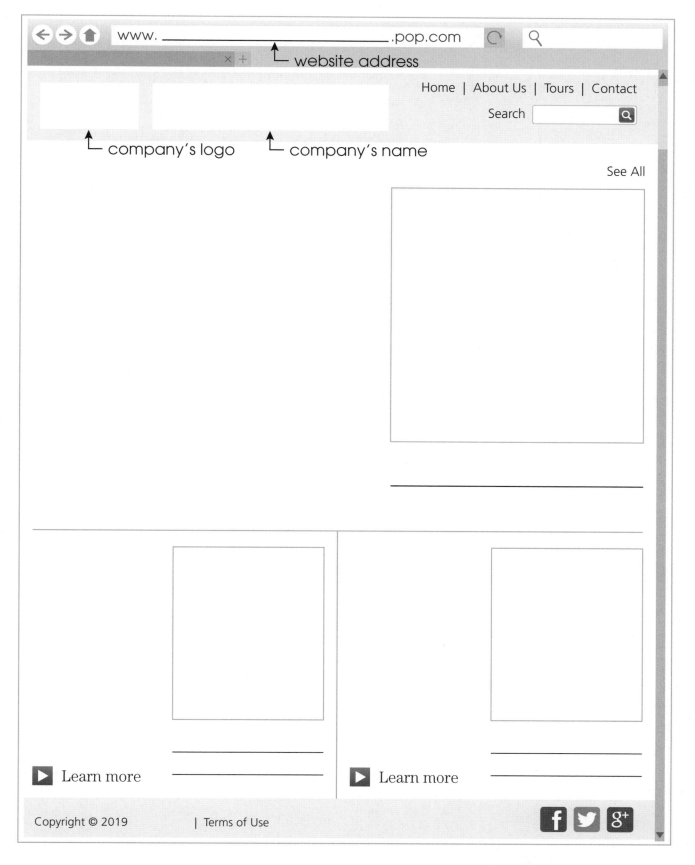

Complete EnglishSmart (Grade 4)

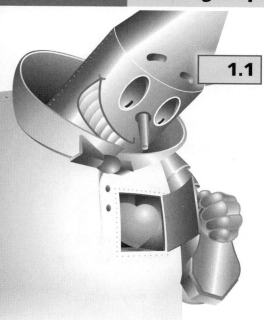

1.1 The Human Heart

The heart is a powerful involuntary muscle that sends blood throughout our body. We cannot control what it does. It sends a single drop of blood around the 100 000 kilometres of blood vessels about a thousand times a day. This is an incredible feat for a muscle that is the size of a human fist.

The heart is made up of four chambers – two at the top and two at the bottom. At the top, the left atrium and the right atrium collect the blood and the bottom two chambers, the ventricles, pump the blood out of the heart. It happens in one single heartbeat for the blood to go from the heart to the lungs where it loads up on oxygen and return to the heart, and then pass all over the body.

To ensure that the blood travels smoothly and consistently, the heart uses valves that open and shut with the flow of blood. The valves only open one way making sure that blood does not re-enter the chambers.

When you are ready for physical action such as running, your heart speeds up and delivers large amounts of oxygen to your legs, enabling you to run quickly. After exercising, you may feel exhausted as your oxygen reserve may be used up. In a few moments, however, you will recover the oxygen needed at rest and your heart will slow down and resume a normal rate. The typical heart rate of an adult is 60 – 80 beats per minute, while a younger heart would beat at a rate of 80 – 100 beats per minute.

1.2

1. What is the heart?

    A. a powerful involuntary muscle

    B. an organ that stores blood

2. Where are the atriums located?

    A. at the top of the heart

    B. at the bottom of the heart

3. Which chambers of the heart collect the blood?

    A. the ventricles

    B. the atriums

4. How do valves make sure that blood does not re-enter the chambers?

    A. They stay shut at all times.

    B. They only open one way.

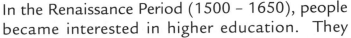

2.1 Education in the Renaissance

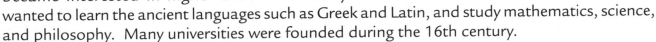

In the Renaissance Period (1500 – 1650), people became interested in higher education. They wanted to learn the ancient languages such as Greek and Latin, and study mathematics, science, and philosophy. Many universities were founded during the 16th century.

University education was a privilege of the rich. Girls were not allowed to attend and poor people could not afford to go. A member of a wealthy family could attend university at the age of ten. He might study at various universities and since the teaching was all done in Latin, it did not matter in which country he studied. It was not unusual for a young boy to study one year in Italy and another in France without speaking either French or Italian.

It was possible in the 16th century to complete university without learning how to read or write. Since books were handwritten, there were not enough to give one to each student. Often, only the teacher had a book. He would read to the students who would memorize what he said. Tests were oral, not written. In fact, many students finished school without ever writing a word!

For the not so wealthy, grammar schools were established in towns. They learned basic grammar and mathematics, and took part in Bible study. At home, girls learned sewing, cooking, dancing, and the basics of taking care of a household. Poor children never attended school.

The Renaissance was a time when scholars did not simply accept what they were told. They conducted scientific experiments in search of answers to the mysteries of the universe. Copernicus calculated that the Earth revolved around the sun but was afraid to publish his works for fear that the Church, who believed in an Earth-centred universe, would punish him. Galileo later supported this theory. The watch, the telescope, and the submarine were some inventions of this period.

2.2

1. What languages did the people in the Renaissance Period learn?

   A. Greek and Latin
   B. French and Italian

2. What did the students learn in grammar schools?

   A. mathematics, science, and philosophy
   B. mathematics, the Bible, and grammar

3. What did girls learn at home?

   A. sewing, dancing, and housekeeping
   B. drawing, painting, and singing

4. What did Copernicus discover about the Earth and the sun?

   A. The Earth revolves around the sun.
   B. The sun revolves around the Earth.

3.1 # J. K. Rowling – Her Story

The success of the Harry Potter books, a fantasy series aimed primarily towards children and young adults, is a modern-day phenomenon. Millions of copies have been sold worldwide.

J. K. Rowling is now enjoying fame and wealth but it was not always that way. When she began to write the first Harry Potter book, she was a single mother of an infant daughter living on social assistance. She lived in a tiny rented apartment in Edinburgh, Scotland. She spent time in a local café where she wrote the first Harry Potter book, *Harry Potter and the Sorcerer's Stone*. This novel completely changed her life.

As a child, J. K. Rowling loved English literature. She wrote her first real story at the age of six. It was then that she decided that she wanted to become a writer. She thought writing would be the best occupation because she would be getting paid to do something she enjoyed.

J. K. Rowling is not absolutely sure where she got the ideas for the Harry Potter stories. The odd names for her characters came from a variety of sources. Some of her characters were loosely based on real people that she knew. However, once she started to develop the characters, they became different from their sources. The Potter series was not based on Rowling's life, although most authors put a little of themselves into their writing.

Through the Harry Potter series, J. K. Rowling has been credited with increasing the interest in reading for children around the world.

3.2

1. What is the target audience of the Harry Potter books?
   A. children and young adults
   B. preschool children

2. Where did J. K. Rowling live when she began to write the first Harry Potter book?
   A. London, England
   B. Edinburgh, Scotland

3. Which occupation did J. K. Rowling think would be best for her?
   A. writing
   B. acting

4. What is J. K. Rowling's Harry Potter series credited for?
   A. increasing the interest in the world of fantasy
   B. increasing the interest in reading for children

4.1 **The Atlas**

An atlas is a scale model of the Earth. It lets us look at the surface of the Earth in its entirety. There are seven large land masses called continents. These include: Africa, Asia, South America, North America, Europe, Antarctica, and Australia. The water surface of the Earth is divided into five oceans: Atlantic, Pacific, Indian, Arctic, and Antarctic.

The imaginary line that circles the globe halfway between the North Pole and the South Pole is called the equator. A similar imaginary line that runs north-south and passes through Greenwich is called the prime meridian. Lines of latitude (called parallels because they run parallel to the equator) run east-west and measure distances north and south of the equator. Lines of longitude (called meridians) run north-south and measure distances east and west of the prime meridian.

Distances on an atlas are measured in degrees (°). Degrees are further divided into minutes. There are 60 minutes for each degree. The equator is at 0° while the North Pole is at 90°. Therefore, the distance from the North Pole to the South Pole is 180° in total. Similarly, the prime meridian is at 0° and distances east and west are between 0° and 180° in both directions for a total of 360° (180° E and 180° W). Therefore, it is easy to plot an exact location on a map. Toronto, for example, is at roughly 44° N and 80° W, and Sydney is at roughly 34° S and 151° E.

4.2

1. Why is an atlas described as "a scale model of the Earth"?

   A. It shows the Earth's seven continents.

   B. It shows the surface of the Earth in its entirety.

2. How many oceans is the Earth's water surface divided into?

   A. five oceans
   B. seven oceans

3. What do the lines of longitude measure?

   A. distances north and south of the equator

   B. distances east and west of the prime meridian

4. What unit is used to measure distances on an atlas?

   A. metre
   B. degree

5.1 Medieval Castles

Medieval castles were built to house the local lords and their families. Inhabitants of the castles usually had their own apartments. Castles were equipped with a nursery, a brewhouse, a school, a chapel, a library, many bedrooms, and an elegant dining room. The dining room was furnished with a grand table for entertaining important guests. Fireplaces were numerous throughout a castle and provided the main source of heat for the apartments. Bedrooms had huge four-poster beds with soft feather pillows and thick curtains to prevent drafts.

The main purpose of a castle was protection. A lord who owned a large amount of land would lease the land out to farmers who would pay him farm produce as rent. He would offer protection against enemy attacks. In the case of an attack, villagers would gather within the castle walls and help defend the castle against invaders. As a result, villages were established near the castle.

Castles were expensive to run. It would cost millions of dollars by today's standards to build and maintain a castle. A noble in medieval times would have an income of about £1000 or US$1500 per year. An ordinary working person might earn the equivalent of one dollar a year. But castle owners had huge expenses. They often employed 300 people to perform various tasks.

In the late 1500s, when battles became large-scale events, castles were not needed. Today, many castles in Europe have been converted into hotels and guesthouses. Many castles are for sale by owners who cannot afford to occupy them. In fact, castles can be purchased for a lot less than you would expect. The real cost comes once you move in and try to pay for the household expenses.

5.2

1. What did the beds in a castle have?
   A. soft leather pillows and thin curtains
   B. soft feather pillows and thick curtains

2. What would farmers do for the lord who leased the land to them?
   A. pay farm produce as rent and help defend the castle
   B. run and maintain the castle

3. What have some castles in Europe been converted into?
   A. hotels and guesthouses
   B. schools

4. Why are many castles for sale?
   A. They are good investments.
   B. They are too expensive for upkeep.

The Incredible Butterfly

R1.1 Butterflies are among nature's most beautiful creations. While their colours have always been admired, particularly by artists, they serve other purposes. Some butterflies use their colours for camouflage. They are able to blend in with tree branches or flowers that they feed on. Some butterflies use their bright colouring as a warning to predators. The Magnificent Owl butterfly has a large dot on each of its wings that looks exactly like an owl's eye. This tricks predators into thinking that the butterfly is a larger animal.

Most butterflies feed on the nectar of plants. They use a long mouthpart called a proboscis to dip into the flowers and suck up the nectar. Some butterflies prefer to feed on rotting fruit. Butterflies are important to nature because they pollinate plants when they feed.

During its life cycle, a butterfly goes through many changes in both body form and colour. There are four stages of butterfly life: egg, caterpillar (larva), chrysalis (pupa), and adult. After about two weeks, baby caterpillars hatch from eggs and start feeding. This stage lasts anywhere from 3 to 12 weeks, depending on the species. The pupa stage is where the caterpillar changes into a butterfly. This transformation takes about two weeks.

Butterflies are found all over the world, but the widest diversity of the species is found in tropical climates. The Painted Lady, which can be found on all continents except Australia and Antarctica, is probably the most widely distributed butterfly in the world.

R1.2

1. Why do artists in particular admire butterflies?
    A. Butterflies have beautiful colours.   B. Butterflies fly among flowers.

2. How do some butterflies defend themselves against predators?
    A. They use their bright colouring as a warning.
    B. They flutter their wings.

3. What does the Magnificent Owl butterfly have that helps protect it against predators?
    A. eyes that look like an owl's eyes   B. a large dot on each of its wings

4. What do most butterflies feed on?
    A. the nectar of plants   B. the water on leaves and flowers

Answers

1   The Human Heart

A. 1. B   2. B
   3. C   4. C
B. 1. A   2. A
   3. B   4. B
C. 1. muscle
   2. vessels
   3. chambers
   4. oxygen
   5. valves
D. 1. The heart consists of four chambers. The left and right atriums collect blood, and the ventricles pump blood out of the heart. The valves control the flow of blood.
   2. One single heartbeat makes blood go from the heart to the lungs where it loads up on oxygen, return to the heart, and then pass all over the body.
   3. When running, the heart speeds up and delivers a lot of oxygen to the legs.
E. (Individual writing)

2   Education in the Renaissance

A. 1. D   2. B
   3. C   4. A
B. 1. A   2. B
   3. A   4. A
C. 1. T   2. F
   3. F   4. T
   5. F   6. T
D. 1. Many universities were founded because people wanted to learn the ancient languages such as Greek and Latin, as well as study mathematics, science, and philosophy.
   2. Inventions from the Renaissance Period include the watch, the telescope, and the submarine.
   3. Copernicus was afraid to publish his works because he feared the Church would punish him.
E. (Individual writing)

3   J. K. Rowling – Her Story

A. 1. D   2. D
   3. C   4. B
B. 1. A   2. B
   3. A   4. B
C. 1. B
   2. E
   3. D
   4. A
   5. C
D. 1. J. K. Rowling wanted to become a writer because she loved English literature and because she would be paid for doing something she enjoyed.
   2. J. K. Rowling came up with the characters by loosely basing them on real people she knew.
   3. (Suggested answer) J. K. Rowling has been credited with increasing children's interest in reading because her fantasy series has sold millions of copies.
E. (Individual writing)

4   The Atlas

A. 1. A   2. A
   3. B   4. B
B. 1. B   2. A
   3. B   4. B
C. Seven Continents: Africa ; Asia ; South America ; North America ; Europe ; Antarctica ; Australia
   Five Oceans: Atlantic ; Pacific ; Indian ; Arctic ; Antarctic
D. 1. The prime meridian is an imaginary line that runs north-south and passes through Greenwich.
   2. The lines of latitude run east-west and measure distances north and south of the equator. The lines of longitude run north-south and measure distances east and west of the prime meridian.
   3. Parallels are the lines of latitude. They are called parallels because they run parallel to the equator.
E. (Individual writing)

5 Medieval Castles

A. 1. B   2. A
   3. A   4. D
B. 1. B   2. A
   3. A   4. B
C. 1. protection
   2. four-poster ; drafts
   3. fireplaces
   4. rent ; produce
   5. battles
D. 1. A medieval castle had a nursery, a brewhouse, a school, a chapel, a library, many bedrooms, and an elegant dining room.
   2. Villages were established near a castle so that they had protection against enemy attacks.
   3. Castles were expensive to run because castle owners had huge expenses and often employed 300 people.
E. (Individual writing)

Review 1

A. 1. They use their colours.
   2. a long mouth
   3. to suck up nectar
   4. the Magnificent Owl
   5. chrysalis
   6. two weeks
   7. in tropical climates
   8. the Painted Lady
B. 1. A   2. A
   3. B   4. A
C.

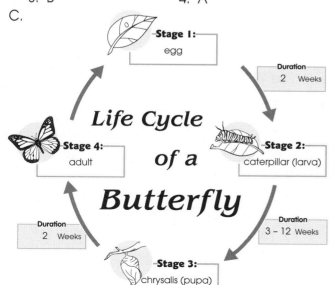

D. 1. They are able to blend in with tree branches or flowers that they feed on.
   2. Butterflies are important to nature because they pollinate plants when they feed.
   3. The pupa stage is where the caterpillar changes into a butterfly.
E. B ; D ; A
   C ; E ; F
F. 1. purposes
   2. continents
   3. pollinate
   4. changes ; colour
   5. proboscis
   6. pupa
G.

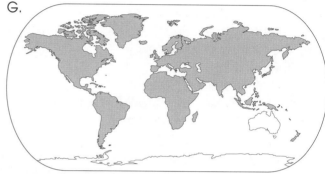

H. 1. Butterflies use their colours for camouflage. They also use their bright colouring as a warning to predators.
   2. There are four stages in a butterfly's life cycle. The first stage is the egg. After about two weeks, the egg hatches and a baby caterpillar is born. After 3 to 12 weeks, it reaches the pupa stage. Then the pupa turns into a butterfly.
I. (Individual writing)

1   Common and Proper Nouns

A. 1. Marie Antoinette
   2. Rosedale
   3. Shih Tzu
   4. Taste Magic
   5. Asia
   6. Stonehenge
   7. Dr. Spinelli
   8. Golden Gate Bridge
   9. Yangtze
  10. Brianna

B. 1. Empire State Building
   2. Art Gallery of Ontario
   3. Where the Wild Things Are
   4. Toronto Maple Leafs
   5. The Chronicles of Narnia
   6. The Lion King
   7. Great Pyramid of Giza

C. Countable Noun: language, fork, apple, cow, house, photo, snowman, toy, octopus
  Uncountable Noun: lightning, love, fire, sugar, music, sand, art, oil, rain, wisdom

(Individual examples)

D. 1. pie
   2. information
   3. music
   4. blocks
   5. popcorn
   6. dishes
   7. salt
   8. soap
   9. seashells

2   Subjects and Objects

A. 1. Hannah
   2. The cat
   3. Joey
   4. We
   5. Recycling
   6. The team's goal
   7. They
   8. Kyle
   9. My favourite teacher
  10. The hockey players

B. 1. trumpet
   2. stars
   3. seat belt
   4. ice cream
   5. books
   6. us
   7. her
   8. children
   9. dog
  10. burgers

C. 1. gardening
   2. many plants
   3. herbs
   4. the plants
   5. some flowers
   6. them
   7. the room
(Individual writing and circling)

D. 1. I
   2. D
   3. D
   4. I
   5. D
   6. I
   7. D
   8. I

3   Pronouns

A. 1. They
   2. We
   3. them
   4. She
   5. her
   6. us
   7. me
   8. I
   9. She
  10. It
  11. him
  12. We

B. 1. yours
   2. mine
   3. ours
   4. theirs

C. 1. mine
2. This present is his.
3. These cards are yours.
4. This bed is theirs.
5. That lunch box is hers.
6. These photo albums are mine.
7. This secret is ours.

D. 1. Which
2. whom
3. What
4. Whose
5. Which
6. Who

E. 1. Who / ~~Which~~ wants to come with me? ◯
2. What / ~~Who~~ has he done to make you angry? ◯
3. With whom / ~~which~~ would you like to dance? ◯
4. I found this key. Whose is it? ✔
5. Which is heavier, a bike or a car? ✔
6. Who / ~~What~~ brought this birthday cake? ◯

F. 1. Who
2. What
3. Who
4. Whose
5. Which
6. Whom
7. Whose
8. Which

G. (Individual questions)

4 Verb Tenses

A. 1. likes
2. says
3. gives
4. takes
5. tries
6. orders
7. likes
8. says
9. hates
10. is
11. is
12. go
13. watches
14. play
15. eat

B. 1. She speaks too loudly in the library. ◯ spoke
2. The kettle whistled when the hot water boiled. ✔
3. Jon writes me a short story. ◯ wrote
4. It takes us three hours to get to the cottage. ◯ took
5. Raindrops fell on my head as I walked home. ✔

C. 1. played
2. decided
3. noticed
4. asked
5. said
6. used
7. lived
8. kept
9. rang

D. 1. will bring
2. will make
3. will come
4. will be
5. will help

E. 1. I will see many clowns at the circus.
2. The soccer game will be exciting.
3. Lindsay will bake an apple pie tomorrow.
4. The Wilson family will go to Italy next week.

returned
F. 1. Gary <u>returns</u> the books to the library last Friday.

will go
2. Maria <u>goes</u> to the musical with her friends tomorrow night.

grows
3. Mom <u>grew</u> a lot of flowers every summer.

did not finish
4. Don <u>will not finish</u> his homework in time for class yesterday.

falls
5. Father's Day <u>fell</u> on the third Sunday of June.

watched
6. We <u>watch</u> the sun set yesterday.

will show
7. I <u>show</u> you the way afterwards.

brought
8. The hurricane <u>brings</u> a lot of rain last week.

Is
9. <u>Was</u> this watermelon sweet?

5   Adjectives

A. 1. more comfortable
2. more difficult
3. worse
4. easier
5. brighter

B. 1. ◯ ; more tiring
2. ✓
3. ◯ ; stronger
4. ✓
5. ◯ ; more interesting

C. 1. taller ; tallest
2. more beautiful ; most beautiful
3. small ; smaller
4. colourful ; most colourful
5. fresh ; fresher
6. more ; most
7. little ; least
8. scary ; scarier
9. more active ; most active

D. (Individual writing)

E. A: (cherry) pie   B: (treasure) chest
C: (fish) bowl   D: (coffee) mug
E: (pencil) sharpener

F. 1. sailing
2. chocolate
3. basketball
4. radio
5. music

G. (Suggested answers)
1. online
2. food
3. alarm
4. hair
5. diamond
6. traffic
7. birthday
8. apple
9. toy
10. cotton
11. pen

6   Adverbs

A. 1. later
2. carelessly
3. hard
4. usually
5. yesterday
6. easily
7. hardly
8. here
9. well
10. wonderfully

B. 1. quickly
2. suddenly
3. awfully
4. cautiously
5. seriously
6. patiently
7. easily
8. solemnly
9. thoughtfully
10. specially

C. more neatly ; higher
better ; sooner
more sweetly ; harder
1. more sweetly
2. harder
3. higher
4. sooner
5. more neatly
6. better

D. 1. more brightly
   2. earlier
   3. more eagerly
   4. nearer
   5. lower
   6. more softly

7　Prepositions

A. 1. across
   2. between
   3. under
   4. by
   5. behind
   6. beside
   7. on
   8. over
B. 1. during
   2. since
   3. on
   4. at
   5. until
   6. on
   7. by
   8. in

C. 1. The mouse scurried (up) the hole in the wall. *toward* ☐
   2. Allison likes strolling (along) the seashore after dinner. ☑
   3. We drove (after) the service station without stopping. *past* ☐
   4. The beautiful island is located one kilometre (along) the coast. *off* ☐
   5. The curious cat chased (after) the chipmunk. ☑
   6. The big snowball rolled (up) the slope at a high speed. *down* ☐
   7. Walking (off) the dense woods can be dangerous. *through* ☐
   8. The koala climbed (up) the tree where its home was. ☑
   9. Willis walked (across) the street to the arcade. ☑

D. (Individual answers)

8　Conjunctions

A. 1. and
   2. but
   3. or
   4. and
   5. and
   6. or
   7. but ; or
   8. and
   9. and
B. (Suggested answers)
   1. The pony eats oats and hay.
   2. Owls and bats sleep during the day and hunt at night.
   3. The days are hot in the summer and cold in the winter.
   4. We can take the midnight flight or the morning flight the next day.
   5. Greg does not like to eat spinach but he likes to eat broccoli.
   6. You can go there to apply in person or you can fill in the form online.
C. 1. Everyone has to wear the seat belt (before) getting into the car. *after* ☐
   2. I always put the toys back in the box (after) I finish playing. ☑
   3. (After) you go to bed, set the alarm clock. *Before* ☐
   4. We helped Mom clean up (before) the guests left. *after* ☐
   5. Give it to the librarian (after) you fill out the form. ☑
   6. (Before) we got on the bus, we showed the transfer tickets to the bus driver. *After* ☐
   7. (After) Emma has touched up the photos, she will send them to me. ☑
   8. We had to go through security check (after) we went on board. *before* ☐

D. (Suggested answers)
1. I should remove the pan from the heat after I have melted the butter, marshmallows, and peanut butter.
2. I should stir in the Rice Krispies after I have removed the pan from the heat.
3. I should butter my hands before I pat down the Rice Krispies in the buttered flat pan.

9 The Sentence: Subject and Predicate

A. Last week, <u>Rita and I</u> went to summer camp. <u>We</u> joined many activities such as swimming, ball games, and talent shows. <u>My favourite activity</u> was arts and crafts. <u>Hats, beaded bracelets, and dreamcatchers</u> were some of the things we made. After the camp, <u>I</u> gave a bracelet to my mom. <u>The bracelet</u> has colourful beads. <u>Mom</u> likes it very much. <u>She</u> wears it all the time.

Subject Noun: My favourite activity ; The bracelet ; Mom
Subject Pronoun: We ; I ; She
Compound Subject: Rita and I ; Hats, beaded bracelets, and dreamcatchers

B. 1. C
2. F
3. A
4. G
5. B
6. D
7. E

C. (Individual compound subjects)
1. (I) like going shopping.
2. (Jill) went to the store.
3. (Charlie) wanted to have pizza for lunch.
4. (My mom) took me to the beach.
5. (His pet dog) slept on the couch in the living room.
6. (Cookies) are Jamie's favourite snacks to eat.
7. (The ducks on the farm) became friends.
8. (The noisy girl) talked and talked during the movie.
9. (The big frog) swallowed the flies around it.
10. (Watermelons) are too sweet for both Grandpa and Grandma.
11. (You) are my best friend in the whole world.
12. (The robots in the toy box over there) belong to Kayla.

D. (Individual writing)

10 Subject-verb Agreement

A. 1. <u>The squirrel</u> (has eaten) our cherries. ; S
2. <u>The hunting dog</u> (is) well trained. ; S
3. <u>The children</u> (were swimming) in the pool. ; P
4. <u>This rabbit</u> always (hides) behind the bushes. ; S
5. <u>Those potatoes</u> (were taken) from Grandpa's farm. ; P
6. <u>These sheep</u> (have) their wool (shorn) by the farmer. ; P
7. <u>The penguins</u> (like) to swim in the ocean. ; P
8. <u>The sun</u> (is shining) brightly in the sky. ; S
9. <u>One of the eggs in the carton</u> (is cracked). ; S
10. <u>The porcelain dolls</u> (were) very expensive and delicate. ; P

B. 1. prepares
2. is

3. are
4. jumps
5. walk
6. has
7. were

C. 1. We ~~is~~ are picking strawberries. ☐

2. The girls ~~plays~~ play soccer together. ☐

3. The flowers are in full bloom. ☑

4. I am going to check the mail. ☑

5. ~~Are~~ Is James working on the assignment? ☐

6. Everyone ~~have~~ has come to celebrate with us. ☐

D. plays ; are ; do ; is ; was ; does ; practises
was ; is ; call ; has ; stick ; like ; enjoys ; are ; love

E. (Individual writing)

11 Simple, Compound, and Complex Sentences

A. 1. S   2. S   3. N
   4. N   5. S

B.

Subject		Predicate
1. The leaves		crawls slowly.
2. The smart child		rattled loudly.
3. The machine		change colour in the fall.
4. Our trip		likes chewing shoes.
5. The snail		solved the puzzle very soon.
6. Kate's puppy		was cancelled because of the bad weather.

C. 1. My computer is old but it still works.
2. The beach is beautiful and it is easy to get to.
3. I will join the party but I have to leave early.
4. My brother is little and he needs to take an afternoon nap.
5. We will watch the football game or we will go out for dinner.
6. Becky needs to study but she has soccer practice.
7. We can have pizza at home or we can eat out.

D. 1. The meeting will be postponed (⟮if⟯ fewer than five members show up).

2. Let's meet at the entrance (⟮before⟯ the game starts).

3. Sophia called Nicole (⟮while⟯ she was waiting for the bus).

4. (⟮When⟯ we arrived in the city), we checked into the hotel first.

5. Tyler never stops practising (⟮unless⟯ he is sick).

6. (⟮Although⟯ the event is over), everyone is still very excited.

7. The family stayed on the farm (⟮until⟯ the sun set).

8. The children play in puddles (⟮whenever⟯ it rains).

E. 1. I tried to keep calm although I was really scared.
2. Handle it with great care since this is the last egg we have.
3. After Randy finished eating his pasta, he would like some desserts.
4. Mom played with me in the park while Dad went to pick up my brother.

12 Phrases and Clauses

A.

	1	2	3	4	5	6	7	8
Phrase		✔		✔			✔	✔
Clause	✔		✔		✔	✔		

B. 1. The little polar bear always climbs on its mother's back.

2. Gilbert did his best in the performance.

3. Joshua is such a helpful person that he drove us home.

4. Do not call me; I will be doing my homework.

5. The flight tickets are expensive during the peak season.

C. 1. A ; (so)
   2. F ; (although)
   3. D ; (because)
   4. E ; (when)
   5. B ; (If)
   6. C ; (and)

D. 1. This boring movie
   2. our mouth-watering dishes
   3. the fluffy creature
   4. great sympathy ; the blind
   5. All of us ; the state-of-the-art cellphone
   6. The appalling living conditions ; this area
   7. Hundreds of people ; free turkeys
   8. The monkey's performance ;
      a lot of applause ; the audience

E. 1. E
   2. D
   3. A
   4. C
   5. B

F. (Individual writing)

| 13 | **More on Phrases** |

A. 1. I wish I (could ride) a real horse. ; ✔
   2. They (should have tidied up) their rooms. ; ✔
   3. We had a barbecue lunch yesterday. ; ✘
   4. You (should keep) an eye on your luggage. ;
      ✔
   5. Uncle Ben (is working) hard on his construction
      project. ; ✔
   6. The Wellings flew to Vancouver last Sunday. ;
      ✘

B. 1. is raining
   2. will visit
   3. were running
   4. have met
   5. had tried
   6. am watching

C. 1. Gosh! The TV (is not working) .
   2. I spend a lot of time working out every day.
   3. Flying kites is their favourite summer activity.
   4. Jumping into the pool is what I want to do
      most.

5. The police (have been looking) into the case
   for months.
6. I (will never forget) walking up the stairs to the
   top of the cathedral.

D. 1. catching the ball
   2. singing loudly
   3. making that noise
   4. Writing a novel
   5. Eating more vegetables

E. 1. The dog in the kennel barked loudly.
   2. Keith was pretty (sure) that was his watch.
   3. The seats on the bus were all occupied.
   4. Mom likes the dress with the (flower) patterns
      best.
   5. The magic show was very (impressive).

F. (Individual writing)

G. 1. for our team
   2. after school
   3. high up
   4. really hard
   5. in the end

H. (Individual writing)

| 14 | **Punctuation** |

A. 1. The movie "Lord of the Rings" ˣwon   ☐
      many Oscarsˣ.
   2. Have you read the book "Cat in the   ✔
      Hat"?
   3. "Beauty and the Beast" is on at the   ☐
      ˣPrincess of Wales Theatreˣ.
   4. ˣMom always watchesˣ "The Basic   ☐
      Chef" for new recipes.
   5. "Finding Nemo" is a ˣpopular movieˣ.   ☐
   6. We can call it "Project X".   ✔
   7. ˣJamie askedˣ, "Where are the keys?"   ☐

B. 1. "Good morning class," said Mrs. Axford.
   2. "Thank you for shopping with us," said the
      salesperson.
   3. Mary shouted, "See you later and have a
      wonderful day!"

C. 1. Tim is a fast runner; he has won many medals.

2. The story is very interesting; I have read it many times.
3. Tomorrow is the last day of school; we need to clear out our lockers.
4. My brother is crazy about SpongeBob; he has T-shirts with the character on them.
5. We are going to the pet store; I want to look at the puppies.

D. Showing Possession: A ; D ; E
Making a Contraction: B ; C ; F ; G

E. 1. Jordan's
2. James's
3. musicians'
4. Suzy's

F. 1. where's
2. I'm
3. doesn't
4. wouldn't
5. there's
6. aren't
7. you're
8. can't
9. isn't
10. mustn't
11. shouldn't
12. she'll

G. (Individual writing)

Review 2

A. 1. <u>Russia</u> is a large country.
2. My cat eats <u>fish</u>.
3. My mom gives <u>me</u> a ring.
4. They
5. fresher
6. most nervous
7. more gracefully
8. until
9. toward
10. along
11. ran all the way home
12. Kelly sings in the shower.
13. The breeze is cool.
14. I love <u>swimming in the morning</u>.
15. Donna walks to school <u>every day</u>.
16. I woke up too early; I am sleepy.

B. live ; belongs ; have ; says ; like ; agrees ; go

C. 1. enjoys

2. ate
3. runs
4. expects
5. scared ; tried
6. laugh

D. (Circle these words.)
Common Nouns (in red): rabbits ; bumblebee ; robin ; middle ; race ; garden ; help ; flowers ; nectar ; family ; help ; worms ; problem ; luck ; flowers ; worms

Proper Nouns (in blue): Buzzer ; Flutter ; Scotch ; Mr. Gregory's ; Buzzer ; Flutter ;Scotch ; Hop

(Underline these words.)
Pronouns: they ; it ; you ; We ; We ; you ; we ; I ; I ; That ; It ; yours ; he ; I ; you ; they

E. (Individual writing)

F. Simple Sentence: 3 ; 8 ; 9
Compound Sentence: 2 ; 4 ; 5
Complex Sentence: 1 ; 6 ; 7

G. 1. C
2. C
3. P
4. P

H. 1. N
2. ADJ
3. V
4. P
5. ADV

I. The three friends arrive at the new garden <u>and</u> they are overjoyed. Not only is there a lot of vegetables <u>but</u> there are many different kinds as well. Hop eats a little of everything. "I (')ll have some lettuce <u>and</u> some cabbage!" he says. (") Look, Buzzer! (") says Hop. "There are many flowers here for you!"

"See all these worms, Flutter?" Buzzer says. "You can have them all!"

(") I (') m so happy I didn (') t win the race today," Hop admits as he, Buzzer, and Flutter relax in the sunshine <u>after</u> their healthful and delicious meal. (") Instead I am able to enjoy all of this with my wonderful friends! (")

1 Adaptation Words

A. behavioural
   evolutionary
   organisms
   environment
   survive
   camouflage
   1. survive
   2. organisms
   3. evolutionary
   4. behavioural
   5. camouflage
   6. environment
B. polar bear
   camel
   stingray
   bat
   goose
C. Behavioural: stingray ; bat ; goose
   Structural: polar bear ; camel
D. (Individual writing)

2 Medical Words

A.

Medical Word / Definition

1. transplant
2. drug
3. doctor
4. hospital
5. sterilized
6. patient
7. infection
8. operation

- a person who practises medicine
- made completely clean and free from bacteria
- caused by germs or bacteria
- a substance used to cure or heal
- a surgical procedure
- replacing a body organ by surgery
- a person receiving medical treatment
- a place where sick people go for care or help

B. (Cross out these words.)
   1. body ; Each word is a medical procedure.
   2. human ; Each word is an organ of the body.
   3. precaution ; Each word means "to make clean".
   4. lawyer ; Each person works in a hospital.

C.

Crossword:
- 1A TRANSPLANT
- B LUNGS
- C HEART
- D REJECTION
- Down 1: INFECTION
- Down 2: SURVIVE
- Down 3: OPERATION
- Across P: PEART
- Down 4: CONGENITAL

D. 1. The (doctor) healed the (patient).
   2. The (ambulance) rushed to the (hospital).
   3. The (heart) (transplant) was successful.
   4. The (surgeon) is performing an (operation).
   5. The (wound) was (sterilized) to prevent (infection).
   6. Taking the (drug) made the man healthy again.

3 Herbal Medicine Words

A. 1. sunflowers
   2. dandelions
   3. aloe vera and jojoba
   4. peppermint
   5. foxglove leaves
   6. the bark of the South American cinchona tree
   7. rosemary
   8. turmeric, boswellia, and licorice
B. 1. medicines
   2. ginseng
   3. Digitalis
   4. foxglove
   5. Quinine
   6. anti-inflammatory
   7. topical
   8. jojoba
C. (Individual answers)
D. 1. aloe vera

2. ginseng
3. dandelion
4. turmeric
5. peppermint
6. foxglove

4 Brain Words

A. 1. the brain
   2. emotion
   3. memory
   4. the nervous system
B. 1. organ
   3. function
   5. cerebrum
   7. hypothalamus
   2. identity
   4. emotions
   6. cerebellum
   8. nervous
C.

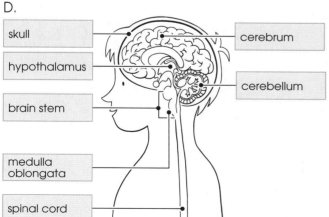

Brain Words

(In red): organ
(In orange): memory
(In brown): hypothalamus
(In pink): functions
(In blue): identity
(In green): cerebrum
(In purple): cerebellum
(In yellow): nervous

D.

skull
hypothalamus
brain stem
medulla oblongata
spinal cord
cerebrum
cerebellum

5 Canadian Words

A. 1. Saskatchewan
   2. Family Day
   3. Louis Riel Day
   4. Prince Edward Island
   5. Islander Day
   6. Canadians
B. (Cross out these words.)
   A: Toronto ; Each word is a Canadian province.
   B: February ; Each word is a Canadian holiday.
   C: Canada ; Each word is a Canadian province.

C.

D.

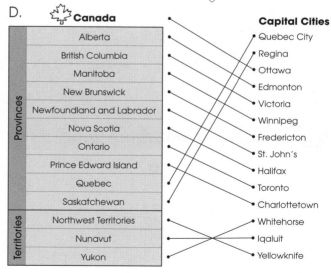

🍁 Canada	Capital Cities
Alberta	Quebec City
British Columbia	Regina
Manitoba	Ottawa
New Brunswick	Edmonton
Newfoundland and Labrador	Victoria
Nova Scotia	Winnipeg
Ontario	Fredericton
Prince Edward Island	St. John's
Quebec	Halifax
Saskatchewan	Toronto
Northwest Territories	Charlottetown
Nunavut	Whitehorse
Yukon	Iqaluit
	Yellowknife

6 Toy and Game Words

A. 1. swing
   2. ball
   3. rag doll
   4. hide-and-seek
   5. hoop rolling
   6. blind man's bluff
   7. wooden soldier
   8. horseshoe pitching
   9. seesaw

B. (Circle these words.)
   creative ; advanced ; interactive ; simple ;
   manufactured ; electronic ; fun ; technical
   1. interactive
   2. simple
   3. electronic
   4. advanced
   5. creative
   6. manufactured
   7. fun
   8. technical

C. (Individual writing)

D. **Toys and Games**

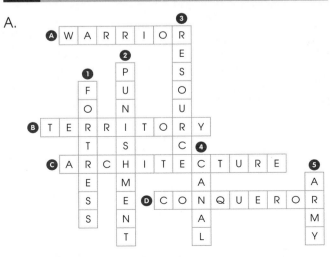

jigsaw puzzle (D)	tug of war (A)
hula hoop (B)	hopscotch (C)

7 Ancient Civilization Words

A.

B. 1. Ancient Rome
   2. Ancient China
   3. Ancient Egypt
   4. Ancient Greece
   5. Ancient Mesopotamia

C. (Circle these words)
   1. highlands
   2. drainage
   3. Mesopotamia
   4. Parthenon
   5. Nile
   6. China
   7. Greece

8 Money Words

A. 1. metal
   2. currency
   3. cheque
   4. barter
   5. debit
   6. jewellery

B. 1. money
   2. beads
   3. feathers
   4. barter
   5. currency
   6. cash
   7. cheque
   8. credit
   9. debit

C. 1.

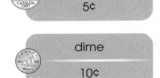 penny* 1¢

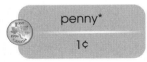 quarter 25¢

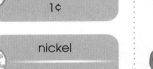 nickel 5¢

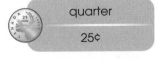 loonie $1

dime 10¢

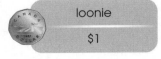 toonie $2

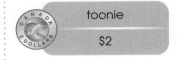

   3. ten-dollar bill ; $10
   4. twenty-dollar bill ; $20
   5. fifty-dollar bill ; $50
   6. hundred-dollar bill ; $100

D.

9   Knight Words

A. (Circle these words.)
1. ceremony
2. Christianity
3. nobleman
4. armour
5. dub
6. oath
7. knight
8. page
9. lance

B. (Cross out these words.)
1. oath
2. nobleman
3. ceremony
(Suggested answers.)
1. Each word is a form of covering or weapon used by a knight.
2. Each word is a level of becoming a knight.
3. Each word is a part of the learning process of becoming a knight

C. 1. squire
2. knight
3. page

D. 1. rituals
2. chapel
3. fasting
4. altar
5. purification
6. knighting
7. lord

10   Weather Words

A. 1. fog
2. sun
3. lightning
4. snow
5. hail
6. breeze
7. frost
8. wind
9. rain

B. 1. D
2. G
3. F
4. H
5. B
6. E
7. A
8. C

C. 1. spring
warm ; grow ; bud
2. summer
hot ; humid ; daylight ; rain
3. fall/autumn
cool ; breezy
4. winter
cold ; dry ; darkness ; snow

D. Precipitation:
drizzle ; freezing rain ; ice pellet ; sleet
Wind:
blast ; draft ; gale ; gust
Extreme Weather Condition:
drought ; heat wave ; hurricane ; ice storm
(Individual words)

11 Sport Words

A. 1. high jump
   2. basketball
   3. soccer
   4. volleyball
   5. badminton
B. 1. athlete
   2. sports
   3. cross-country
   4. volleyball
   5. basketball
   6. badminton
   7. Track and field
   8. shot put
   9. high jump
   10. soccer

C.

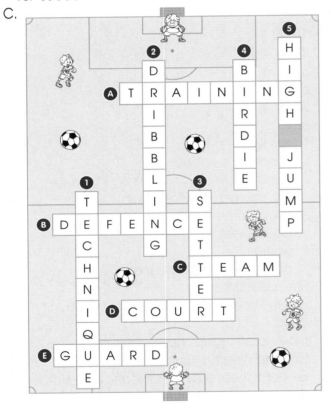

D.

More Sports   **Sport Equipment**

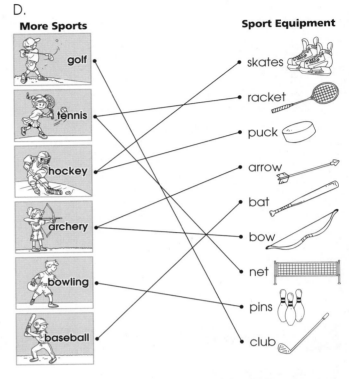

12 Gardening Words

A. 5 ; plants
   6 ; fruit
   1 ; nursery
   4 ; mulch ; soil
   2 ; compost ; manure
   3 ; sunlight
B. 1. F
   2. C
   3. E
   4. B
   5. G
   6. A
   7. D

C. 1. root
2. fruit
3. leaf
4. flower
5. stem
6. seed
7.

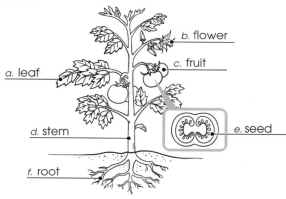

b. flower
c. fruit
a. leaf
d. stem
e. seed
f. root

D. 1. rake
2. gloves
3. hose
4. lawn mower
5. watering can
6. trowel ; pruners

13 Musical Instrument Words

A. 1. trumpet
2. flute
3. drums
4. saxophone
5. piano
6. violin
7. trombone
8. clarinet

B. Woodwind ; C ; F ; I
Brass ; D ; H
String ; A ; B
Percussion ; E ; G

C. 1. harp
2. maracas
3. recorder
4. French horn
5. triangle
6. lyre

Brass: 4   Percussion: 2, 5
String: 1, 6   Woodwind: 3

14 Technology Words

A.

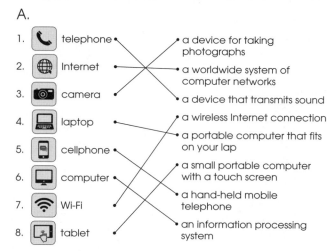

1. telephone — a device that transmits sound
2. Internet — a worldwide system of computer networks
3. camera — a device for taking photographs
4. laptop — a portable computer that fits on your lap
5. cellphone — a hand-held mobile telephone
6. computer — an information processing system
7. Wi-Fi — a wireless Internet connection
8. tablet — a small portable computer with a touch screen

B. Past: Walkman ; cassette ; typewriter
Present: tablet ; Wi-Fi ; e-reader
Both: television ; computer ; telephone ; radio

C.
1. television
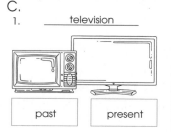
past | present

2. telephone
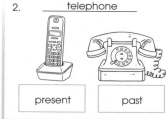
present | past

3. camera
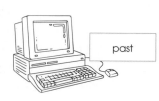
present | past

4. computer
past

5. cellphone
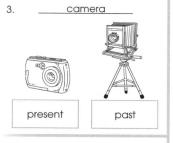
present | past

present

D. 1. computer
2. Internet
3. Wi-Fi
4. router
5. modem
6. camera
7. e-reader

Review 3

A. 1. jewellery
   2. an adaptation
   3. a seesaw
   4. camouflage
   5. drainage
   6. hopscotch
   7. a fortress
   8. oath of chivalry
   9. habitat
   10. a wooden soldier
   11. compost
   12. a squire
   13. a canal
   14. currency
   15. a predator
   16. an armour

B. 1. The wound was not properly disinfected.
   2. Congenital diseases can lower defence.
   3. The brain is a vital organ.
   4. The surgeon operated on her spinal cord.
   5. The infection has spread to his lungs.
   6. The cerebellum of birds is highly developed.
   7. Susie's loss of memory destroyed her identity.
   8. The doctor prescribed vitamins to strengthen the nervous system.

   Brain Word: brain ; surgeon ; spinal cord ;
   cerebellum ; memory ;
   nervous system

   Medical Word: wound ; disinfected ;
   congenital ; infection ; lungs

C. computer ; camera ; router ; Wi-Fi ; tablet ;
   clarinet ; drums ; guitar ; violin ; trumpet/trombone ;
   athlete ; soccer ; tennis ; volleyball ; cross-country

D. Provinces: Alberta
   British Columbia
   Manitoba
   New Brunswick
   Newfoundland and Labrador
   Nova Scotia
   Ontario
   Prince Edward Island
   Quebec
   Saskatchewan

   Territories: Northwest Territories
   Nunavut
   Yukon Territory

E. 1. lightning ; rain
   2. fog
   3. wind
   4. hail

F.

	❶						
	F		❷				
Ⓐ	L	E	A	F		❸	
	O	Ⓑ	R	O	O	T	
	W		U			R	
Ⓒ S	T	E	M	I		E	
	R		T	Ⓓ	S	E	E	D

G.

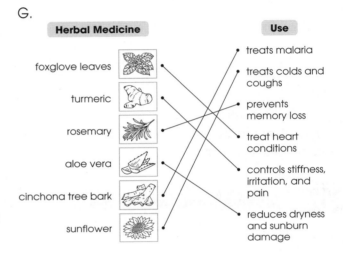

Herbal Medicine		Use
foxglove leaves		treats malaria
turmeric		treats colds and coughs
rosemary		prevents memory loss
aloe vera		treat heart conditions
cinchona tree bark		controls stiffness, irritation, and pain
sunflower		reduces dryness and sunburn damage

1 Not a Typical Grandma

A. 1. Grams
   2. not typical
   3. when she swims
   4. in Australia
B. 1. The purpose of this letter is to show how Emily's grandma is not a typical grandma.
   2. Emily's grandma loves rollerblading, whitewater rafting, mountain climbing, and tobogganing.
   3. (Suggested answers)
      over the hill: old
      dressed to the nines: dressed very glamorously
      ants in your pants: restlessness
      go like the wind: go fast
      greatest thing since sliced bread: the best ; very cool
C. (Individual writing)
D. (Individual writing)

2 Camp Wannastay

A. 1. unknown
   2. Steve
   3. one week
   4. first place
B. 1. It is a diary.
   2. It consists of entries organized in chronological order. Each entry has the date at the top and usually begins with "Dear Diary".
   3. The writer thinks that the camp counsellor is the coolest because he organized cooperative games for the campers to get to know one another on the second day.
C. (Individual writing)
D. (Individual writing)

3 The Father, the Son, and the Donkey

A. 1. to sell it
   2. no one
   3. a woman
   4. a pole and some strings
B. 1. The crowd jeered at the man and his son because they were both riding the donkey, which was struggling to carry them both.
   2. The problem is that the man and his son cannot please the strangers.
   3. The moral of the story is that it is impossible to please everyone.
C. (Individual writing)
D. (Individual writing)

4 A Pet's Tale

A. 1. a dog
   2. in a pet store
   3. She is busy.
   4. a retired lady
B. 1. The pet thinks it is lucky because it gets adopted.
   2. She treats the pet like a queen.
   3. (Suggested answers)
      1st Stanza: excited
      2nd Stanza: disappointed
      3rd Stanza: sad
      4th Stanza: happy
C. 1. more
   2. bone
   3. shared
   4. free
   5. daughter
   6. owner
   7. mend
   8. alone
   9. other
   10. queen
D. bright ; night ; sleep ; cheep
E. (Individual writing and drawing)

5   A Rebus Invitation

A. 1. a birthday party
2. in the afternoon
3. outdoors
4. lunch

B. 1. It uses letters, pictures, and words to convey a message. (Suggested examples) Jul 👁 and ☕🍰.
2. Paragraph 1: It gives the details of the birthday party, including, the date, time, and location. Paragraph 2: It tells what food will be served. Paragraph 3: It tells what to bring to the birthday party.
3. They need to bring sunscreen and bug spray.

C. Dear Carlos,
You are invited to my birthday party on Sunday, July 12. It starts at two o'clock and ends at five o'clock. We will meet at the Wheeler Horse Farm on Queen Street.
Lunch will be hot dogs, french fries, and cupcakes.
Please bring sunscreen and bugspray.
Your friend,
Shelley

D. (Individual writing)

E. (Individual writing)

6   New France – the Beginning of Canada

A. 1. Jacques Cartier
2. in Montreal
3. in Quebec City
4. in 1774

B. 1. It is useful because readers can understand history in chronological order.
2. The English and the French fought over the new territory, New France, in 1759.
3. They allowed the French to maintain their culture, religion, traditions, and language under British rule.

C. (Individual writing)

D. (Individual writing and drawing)

7   Seal Island

A. 1. in South Africa
2. from February to September
3. by boat
4. crabs, squid, and fish

B. 1. Yes, it is a brochure because it is a piece of folded paper that is advertising a travel destination: Seal Island.
2. It is from the company Seal Island Adventures.
3. Great White Sharks camouflage themselves against the dark, rocky bottom of the sea and then breach and strike the seals.
4. It is the area surrounding Seal Island where the sharks attack the seals. It is called "the ring of peril" because the seals risk their lives each time they leave the island.

C. 1. Amazing Seal Island
2. See the seals, See the sharks, See South Africa!
3. Where, What, When, Weather, How
4. There are images of seals, a shark, a map, a graph, and the company logo.
5. Seals in the sun
6. Seal Island Adventures
7. sealislandadventures@pop.com ; 123-456-7891
8. www.si-a.com

D. (Individual writing)

E. (Individual design and writing)

8   The Production of Milk

A. 1. two times
2. below 4°C
3. by automatic packaging machines
4. in refrigerated rooms

B. 1. The diagram shows the stages of the milk production process.
2. Milking cows in the past was done by hand. Today, milking machines are used to milk cows.
3. Milk is stored in refrigerated silos and then pasteurized and homogenized.

C. 1. Milk Production Process
2. pasture ; milking machine ; silos ; tanker ; processing factory ; packaging machine ; refrigerated room
3. boxes ; illustrations

D. (Individual writing)

E. (Individual design and writing)

9   Salamanders

A. 1. an amphibian
   2. warm climates
   3. through their skin
   4. 19
B. 1. The topic is salamanders.
   2. It has a long body that is roundish in the centre with four limbs and a tail. Its round eyes have eyelids and it has no eardrums or claws.
   3. It has three pairs of red gills on each side of its head.
   4. In spring, a salamander migrates to a pond where it deposits its eggs in a little bundle or a larger oval mass. A larva feeds on other animals. It turns into an adult salamander by the end of summer.
C. 1. Amphibians
   2. Salamanders
   3. The Mud Puppy ; The Life Cycle
   4. There is a diagram of a salamander's anatomy, as well as a life cycle diagram.
D. (Individual writing)
E. (Individual writing and drawing)

10   Disasters at Sea

A. 1. in 1912
   2. to New York City
   3. 1477
   4. the Lusitania
B. 1. It is non-fiction because the text is based on real shipwrecks.
   2. (Suggested answers)
      The Titanic: It struck an iceberg and plunged into the sea in less than three hours.
      The Empress of Ireland: It was rammed by a Norwegian coal ship in thick fog and sank in 14 minutes.
      The Lusitania: It was torpedoed by a German submarine and sank in 18 minutes.
C. 1. Disasters at Sea
   2. The Titanic ; The Empress of Ireland ; The Lusitania
   3. picture ; map
   4. The Titanic's route map ; The Lusitania before sinking

5. cause and effect, compare and contrast, and time order or sequence
   6. (Individual answer)
D. (Individual writing)
E. (Individual writing and drawing)

11   The Case of the Disappearing Fish

A. 1. three
   2. in the suburbs
   3. in his pond
   4. devastated
B. 1. The topic is on some missing pet fish.
   2. His backyard has a garden and a pond with a beautiful waterfall.
   3. They were suspects because one of them threatened to release José's fish and frogs into a natural habitat, while the other threatened to eat José's fish and frogs.
   4. It was a large bird.
C. 1. August 14, 2019
   2. Prized Pet Fish Missing from Backyard Pond
   3. By Percival O'Brien
   4. 1
   5. 2 ; 3; 4
   6. "When I saw the size of the bird, my eyes widened in disbelief. I cannot believe that I was completely wrong the entire time."
   7. The pond in José's backyard, where three fish have gone missing
D. (Individual writing)
E. (Individual writing and drawing)

12 Being the Eldest

A. 1. Evan Smith
2. Kids Advice Magazine
3. Evan
4. his toys

B. 1. It is formal because it is addressed to a professional advice magazine.
2. The subject is: Advice for My Sibling Situation.
3. The purpose is to seek advice on how Evan can deal with his two younger siblings who are always bothering him.
4. (Suggested answers)
Reason 1: Evan's siblings are always asking to play with him and his friends.
Reason 2: Evan has to eat everything on his plate during mealtimes, whereas his siblings do not.

C.

D. (Individual writing)
E. (Individual writing)

13 Nature's Fireworks

A. 1. Latin
2. a natural light phenomenon
3. the southern lights
4. in the North

B. 1. The topic is aurora borealis.
2. They are created by particles from the sun that collide with different gases in Earth's atmosphere.
3. The Inuit of Alaska: They believed that the lights were the spirits of the animals they hunted.
The Menominee of Wisconsin: They regarded the lights as torches used by great, friendly giants in the North to help them spear fish at night.
Other Aboriginal peoples: Some believed that the lights were the spirits of their people, and some an omen of war.

C. 1. aurora borealis
2. Myths and Legends
3. photo
4. Aurora borealis in Whitehorse, Yukon, Canada

D. (Individual writing)
E. (Individual writing and drawing)

14 Stonehenge

A. 1. around 5000 years ago
   2. where it was built
   3. sarsen stones
   4. lintels
B. 1. The purpose is to provide information about Stonehenge.
   2. Stonehenge is a formation of large stones arranged in a ring.
   3. The sarsen stones are the largest stones in the outer ring of the formation. They are nearly three stories tall, each weighing more than three African elephants.
   4. The stones are arranged so that they line up with the sunrise during the summer solstice.
C. 1. Stonehenge Uncovered
   2. Stonehenge ; What is it? ; What happens twice a year?
   3. a photograph/picture of Stonehenge
   4. Stonehenge in Wiltshire, England
   5. (Check these circles.) links ; search box ; footer ; main menu bar ; paragraphs ; navigation buttons ; audio or video
   6. (Check these circles.) copyright symbol with year ; terms of use ; social media links
D. (Individual writing)
E. (Individual design and writing)

Review 4

A. 1. date, greeting, signature
   2. in chronological order
   3. at the end
   4. talking animals
   5. paragraphs
   6. late, fate, bell, spell
   7. a rebus
   8. **1956** – started school
      1958 – first vacation
      1961 – sister born
   9. advertises products
   10. a vacation
   11. a flow diagram
   12. to provide information
   13. @
   14. an informational text
   15. a caption
   16. a timeline
   17. a diary
B. 1. T
   2. T
   3. F
   4. F
   5. T
C. 1. (Suggested features)
      It is a newspaper article.
      Features: a headline, a quote
   2. The cornfield cracked open, and smoke and ash began to spew. The next day the mound of earth continued to grow shooting up rocks and lava, and spreading over the cornfield.
   3. It means when the volcano stops growing.
   4. He says it is an opportunity because he is able to study the birth, growth, and death of a volcano.
   5. The volcanic eruption destroyed San Salvador Paricutín and the neighbouring village of San Juan, and volcanic ash had choked surrounding forests.
   6. (Individual answer)
D. (Individual writing and drawing)
E. (Individual writing and drawing)

1.

<u>I</u> <u>HAVE</u> <u>HAD</u>

<u>GREAT</u> <u>FUN</u> <u>HERE</u>

<u>AND</u> <u>I</u> <u>WILL</u> <u>VISIT</u>

<u>YOU</u> <u>AGAIN</u>

<u>NEXT</u> <u>YEAR</u>.

2.

fish	puck	book	star
(rich)	duck	look	jar
squish	truck	hook	(store)
dish	luck	(lock)	bar
wish	(neck)	cook	car

3.

b a n d

b e n d

b o n d

b o n e

c o n e

t o n e

t u n e

4.

Months

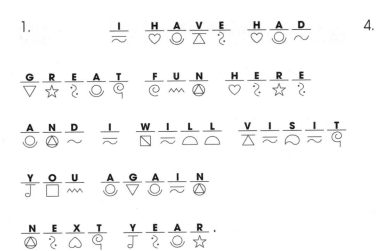

5. 1. STEAL 2. THINK
3. SCARCE 4. SEAT
5. CHIEF 6. FLIGHT
7. GRAIN 8. EXITS/EXIST
9. SWING 10. REPLY

6.

soccer ball — csocre lbla

basketball — askalbetlb

volleyball — oleyvlalbl

hockey puck — okhcye ukcp

baseball — aallsbeb

football — footaoll

golf ball — ofgl lalb

tennis ball — sentin abll

shuttlecock — httsleucokc

7.

Crossword:
- e l v e s o x
- e h e r o e s n
- s e c c
- e e h i
- g c i t
- n i m n e r d i
- e e s
- m e s o o m r e e d

8.

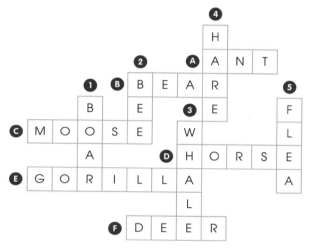

- H A N T
- B E A R
- B E E
- C M O O S E
- D H O R S E
- E G O R I L L A
- F D E E R
- F L E A

9. A. I prefer to sleep on rocks.
B. I love jumping out of the water.
C. I like to stay on the ocean floor.
D. I would rather swim across the ocean all day.

10.

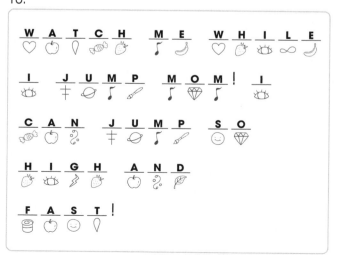

WATCH ME WHILE
I JUMP MOM! I
CAN JUMP SO
HIGH AND
FAST!

11.

wind
wand
sand
said
sail

12.

Australia, Canada, North America, Africa, China, South America, Antarctica, Europe, Russia, Asia

13.

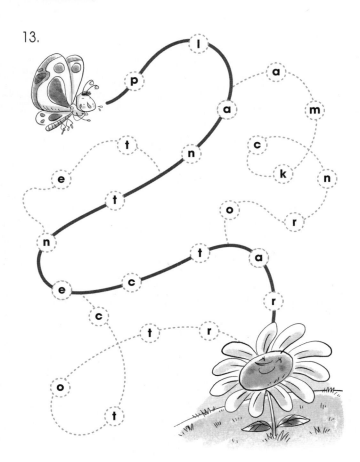

Language Games

1 Decode and write what Mokki the Alien is saying to the children.

Decoded message:

I HAVE HAD GREAT FUN HERE AND I WILL VISIT YOU AGAIN NEXT YEAR.

Cipher key:

A	B	C	D	E	F	G	H	I	J	K	L	M
◎	⸾	△	~	⸮.	@	▽	♡	≈	⌣	⌀	⌒	✪

N	O	P	Q	R	S	T	U	V	W	X	Y	Z
◬	□	⍓	≀	☆	⌒	℺	⋙	◿	⊿	♡	♩	⩘

2 Circle the word that does not rhyme in each group.

share

pear

tear

bear

chair

fish	puck	book	star
rich	duck	look	jar
squish	truck	hook	store
dish	luck	lock	bar
wish	neck	cook	car

3 Help the band play a tune by changing one letter in the word each time.

| b | a | n | d |

| b | | n | d |

| b | | n | d |

| b | o | n | |

| | o | n | e |

| | o | n | e |

| | t | n | e |

4 Circle the 12 months of the year in the word search.

| January | February | March | April | May | June |

| July | August | September | October | November | December |

Months

J	U	N	E	✿	S	V	P	W	X	U	M	A	Y	📚
🎄	N	E	R	T	R	🏰	Q	D	A	B	💘	U	F	G
S	C	O	X	Z	L	M	F	E	B	R	U	A	R	Y
E	J	A	V	D	J	I	O	C	T	O	B	E	R	C
P	T	O	N	E	U	Y	F	E	A	L	O	🍁	J	C
T	K	L	☂	N	M	H	☀	M	D	F	N	A	E	T
E	B	R	O	K	Y	B	M	B	E	P	J	U	L	Y
M	A	R	C	H	H	L	E	E	C	B	🍀	G	Q	S
B	P	🍦	J	A	N	U	A	R	Y	E	T	U	W	O
E	A	T	N	Z	M	L	🎃	I	G	R	A	S	U	V
R	T	U	V	⛄	A	P	R	I	L	M	A	T	L	K

5 Help Jerry insert the letter cards into the words in the word machine to form new words.

1. **T** SEAL

2. **K** THIN

3. **C** SCARE

4. **A** SET

5. **I** CHEF

6. **L** FIGHT

7. **R** GAIN

8. **S** EXIT

9. **W** SING

10. **P** RELY

Word Machine

Insert

New Words

New Words

1.   STEAL   2. _____

3. _____   4. _____

5. _____   6. _____

7. _____   8. _____

9. _____   10. _____

6 Unscramble the letters to help the goalie write the names of the sports equipment.

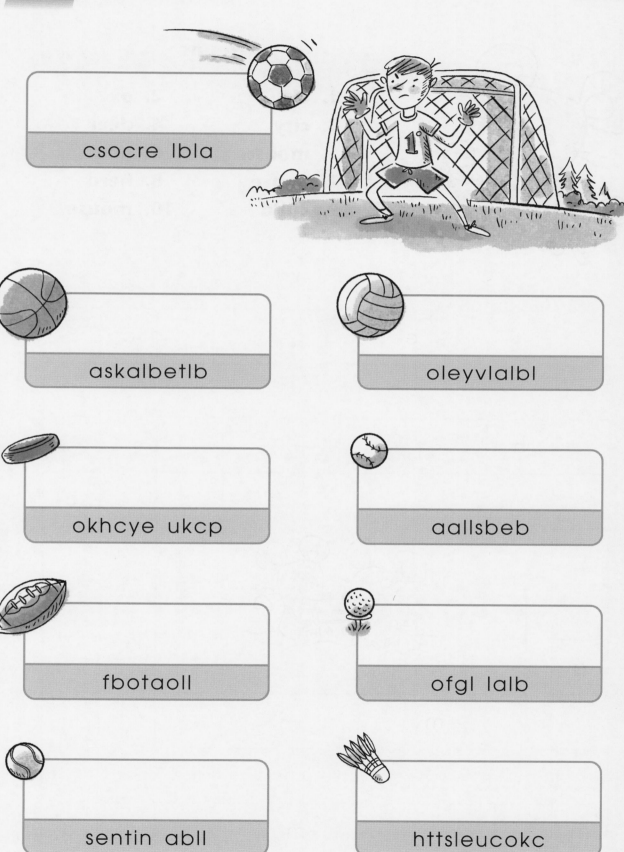

csocre lbla

askalbetlb

oleyvlalbl

okhcye ukcp

aallsbeb

fbotaoll

ofgl lalb

sentin abll

httsleucokc

7 Help Marco the Mouse get to the centre of the maze to meet his friends. Write the plural of each noun.

Nouns

1. elf	2. ox
3. city	4. deer
5. moose	6. man
7. goose	8. hero
9. child	10. mouse

8 Complete the crossword puzzle with a homophone for each clue word. Each answer is an animal word.

Across

- A aunt
- B bare
- C mousse
- D hoarse
- E guerrilla
- F dear

Down

- 1 bore
- 2 be
- 3 wail
- 4 hair
- 5 flee

9 Unscramble what the sea creatures say.

A *prefer on rocks the sleep I to .*

B *water the jumping I out of love !*

C *like stay ocean on I floor the to .*

D *rather would I all day swim across the ocean .*

A _____

B _____

C _____

D _____

10 Decode and write what Ken the Kangaroo is saying to his mother.

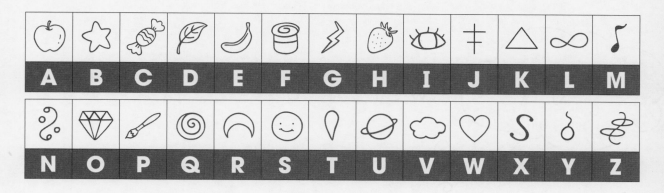

11 Show how the wind makes the boat sail by changing one letter in the word each time.

| w | i | n | d |

| w | | n | d |

| | a | n | d |

| s | a | | d |

| s | a | i | |

12 Help the dog catch the Frisbees by colouring the Frisbees that have continent words.

Australia

Canada

North America

Africa

China

South America

Antarctica

Europe

Russia

Asia

13 Help Betty the Butterfly find the flower by tracing the path following the letters in the words "plant nectar".

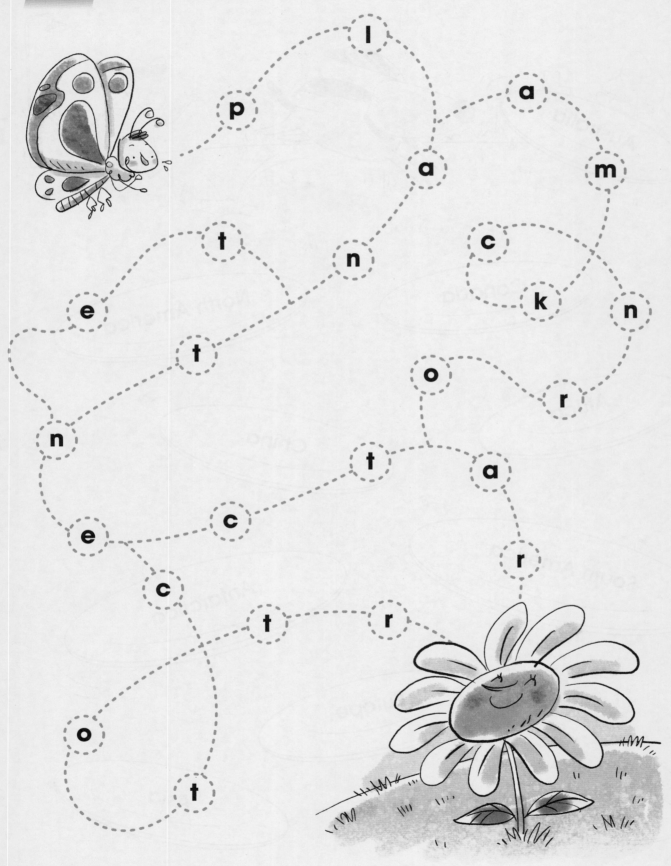

Language Game

DESIGN Challenge

We have an exciting Language Game Design Challenge! Submit your design to win a prize if your entry is selected and posted on our website!

Entry Rules:

- You have a passion for learning English.
- *Complete EnglishSmart* is your favourite learning tool.
- You are between 6 and 14 years old.

How to Enter:

1. Use the back of this page to create your own language game.
2. Give your language game a title.
3. Make sure the language game is fun!

My Contact Information

Name: _____ Age: _____

School: _____ Grade: _____

E-mail: _____

Parent's Signature

Scan and e-mail this form and your language game to: *ca-info@popularworld.com* or mail it to: 15 Wertheim Court, Units 602-603, Richmond Hill, Ontario, Canada L4B 3H7.